THE CIRCLE IS COMPLETE

Dear Sue —
   Thanks for all your support and kindness.
   It encouraged me to complete this 1st Part of my story

Bonnie

THE CIRCLE IS COMPLETE

AN ADOPTION AND REUNION STORY PART ONE-CAT

BONNIE L. QUICK

This is a story based on the truth. Some names and locations have been changed to protect people not directly involved in the story.

PREFACE

The Circle is Complete Volume One--CAT is an updated version of a book I started to write several years ago after my reunion with my daughter in 1991. I had given up for adoption in the 1960s. By now, Cat and I have known each other for more years than we have not. Part of this book is about finding her—or rather her finding me but it is mostly about the development of a relationship between a birth mother and an adoptee including all the peripheral relationships a story like this entails.

Along the way are adventures, disappointments, surprises, reprisals and every other thing you would expect from a deeply personal story that so many people can identify with.

The rules and regulations of adoption and reunion have changed drastically since the 60s when my story began. In addition, it took many years of covering up the shame and self blame of also having a son born in the early 1960s before I was ready to reveal that fact. Three years before Cat, I had a brief encounter that ended in a pregnancy. I gave birth to my son two months before my 19th birthday. And as was the custom at that time for white middle class unmarried females, the choices were get married or give up the baby for adoption.

John found me about ten years after Cat did we also began a relationship in the early 2000s.

John's story will be more completely covered in Volume Two.

During the years from the 60s to late 80s the key thing I felt about being a birth mother aside from the hurt and sense of loss I lived with everyday was the deep remorse and sense of shame I felt over the decisions I felt forced to make.

No doubt the impact of giving up two children to be raised by other people colored my life considerably, that I spent much energy trying to hide what I had been through to the detriment of my own mental health and ruination of a number of relationships. I did not turn to drugs as my comfort in order to make it through each day, but that in itself seems miraculous and can only thank God.

I needed approval and spent a huge amount of time in the first years after I gave up my son to prove I was okay and could be an acceptable partner. I majored on keeping men at a distance. I dated a lot of guys, but had no intimate relationships for a long time. I took pride in the fact that I could keep a man's attention without even having to kiss him good night. As I look back over my life I realize that I used my relationships with men as a panacea, a cure all believing that if one of them would love me, I must be okay and could forgive myself.

I realize how sick and wounded I was. I expended a huge amount of energy presenting myself as a "GOOD Girl" which in the early sixties meant I did not have intercourse. In those days, I did not even think or conceptualize the idea of oral sex. I must have been in my mid twenties before I even had that particular type to sexual activity on my radar screen.

Deep inside I saw myself as damaged goods and did not feel

completely comfortable with any sexual activity, although I liked how it felt when I was kissed passionately or had my breasts touched. Below the belt was totally taboo until the one guy I could not resist.

I have no idea why him but I found it tough to keep my hands off him and invited his touch. At the same time I am sure I drove him crazy because half the time I was pushing him away and the other half I was calling him close.

At that time in my life I was still trying to work up the courage to think about sex without marriage. I did not think it was normal to do sex and the one man I slept with was a secret for a long time. He turned out to be the father of my daughter that I have written this book about.

When I attempt to talk to people raised in other eras, they no longer condemn me for getting pregnant without marriage, yet I sense I am being judged for choosing to allow my kids to be brought up in a "complete family"

As I say, so incredibly different were social mores and expectations for 1963. Working on this book has made me revisit a bunch of things I never wanted to look at. Similar to the woman who has been raped, the victim wants justice, but is not really prepared to walk through the event that so trauma-tized her.

That is true no matter what the trauma. There is loss and grief through the healing process. Shame, Fear, and so many other emotions dip in and out of the conscious or subconscious mind. A smell, a color, temperature, place, time of day or year, song, food… The things that trigger a flashback are as varied as the individual dealing with it.

To my friends too numerous to name, who were always available to me, thanks. To the members of my family who supported me, thanks.

A special Thank You to Cheri who held my hand just at the right time.

PROLOGUE

I feel it is only fair to allow you readers to share the entire text of the letter that changed so many lives and inspired me to write this book. It arrived at my home at an utterly unexpected time. Twenty-four years after the fact.

I guess I had stopped hoping. But there it was, in black and white.

April 19, 1991

Dear Bonnie,

This is the most important letter I have ever had to write. I am not sure of what to say or how to say it, but I will try my best to make some sense.

My name is Cathy. I was born Jane Hilarie (sic) XXXXXX 11-1-66 in Elk County Hospital, Ridgway (sic), PA. I was placed in foster care 11-3-66. *Five months later, I was adopted by Robert and Rosemarie XXXXX. I was raised in Bethlehem, PA, with my sister Caryl, who is eight years my senior. My family was middle class, comfortable, and normal. I have been healthy and happy.*

My husband, Steve, and I are expecting our first child in May. Even though I have had no serious health problems, I am interested in my medical background to ensure my health and the baby's. I have been conducting a search for you since July. I had thought about it for years but did not feel the "need" until I learned I was pregnant. I explored several different avenues and all my evidence pointed to you. (I just found your address last night!)

The Photo CAT sent with her letter to me.

I realize what a shock this is. I have had the advantage of mentally preparing for this moment. I would like to assure you that I do not wish to disrupt your life in any way. I would not involve any one else, or cause you any embarrassment. I am ashamed to admit a few white lies were told to locate you. I felt it was necessary to protect your confidentiality. I hope you will not resent this or those people who helped supply your address.

I understand I have a sister and a brother and I realize what a delicate situation this is. Please understand I have many personal questions as well as medical. What I seek is an adult relationship. I would be receptive to a possible friendship. Once more I want to stress that this is not an attempt to complicate your life. I will not pursue this issue if you are not comfortable. If that is the case, I would appreciate a little family history such as my heritage and diseases or disorders.

Being due in four weeks, I am home most of the time! You may call me at 215 XXX-XXXX anytime. I hope all this makes sense. I am very emotional at this time and I am sure I forgot to include a lot of things. It's hard to cram 24 years onto two pieces of paper. My picture is enclosed.

THANK YOU,

. . .

3

BONNIE L. QUICK

CATHY

   XXX Street
   Bethlehem, PA 18018

1

THE LETTER

It was April and a beautiful day in Northwest Florida. The mail lady in her little red, white, and blue truck came driving down the tree lined rural dirt road. It seemed to be a day like any other. We waved at each other.

My mother was visiting and my daughter was in school. For some reason, I was not working that day. I strolled lazily to the mailbox located a half acre away enjoying the spring blossoms and warm sunshine. It was, weather-wise, a perfect day, the kind you hear people ordering in the midst of either a very cold winter or a very hot summer.

Temperate, I guess you would call it. I was not expecting anything of any consequence, so I was not prepared for what was in the mailbox.

At first it looked innocent enough, a business-sized envelope with handwriting that I did not recognize. I was accustomed to hearing from strangers about one thing or another since I knew many people and was on committees, taught classes, and counseled clients, etc. I was fairly visible in the small community.

As I stood in the road opening the envelope, a picture jumped out at me. It was a beautiful young woman. At first I thought it was one of the young ladies from my single parent class but at a closer look I realized it was not Celina.

It was obviously a wedding dress the young woman was wearing, and the face was somehow vaguely familiar. I studied the photograph for a moment and thought her very intriguing. I anxiously began to read the letter. As I got past the first sentence, I felt weak in the knees and tears began to flow freely from my eyes. Was I even breathing? It was as if time had stopped. There was no feeling in my body.

The letter started *"This is the most important letter I have ever had to write."* From there it went to *"I was born Jane Hilarie XXXXX on November 1, 1966..."* It was my daughter who I had given up for adoption at birth so long ago! I turned over the page to see if there was a phone number. I could not read the rest of the words for a few moments. I stood in the yard looking up at the tall pine trees, searching for strength. Surely there was some wisdom to be found in the surrounding nature. It was a miracle, but I was scared. It was almost too much to hope for.

Not for an instant did I consider not responding. It was like my heart instantly took on a new shape as the big empty space filled in. I only wanted to get to her.

"Continue, be brave, keep going", I said over and over to myself...And now the day had come. She wanted to know me. Shocking! Exhilarating! Terrifying!

I walked into the house. I handed my mother the photograph.

She asked, *"Who is that?"*

I said, *"It is my daughter".*

'But, you had a son."

I repeated, *" This is my daughter."*

My mother said *"What?"* (It sounded more *like "whaaaaat?"*)

I repeated. *"That is my daughter".*

My mother was totally shocked since she did not know I had a baby while she and my father were living outside the United

States, in Germany. Cat was born in Pennsylvania and I never spoke of it.

I went for the telephone. I do not remember my conversation with my mother. I dialed the number and it was busy. I started to read the letter again.

"This is the most important letter I have ever had to write".

She wrote that her name was Cathy. She was pregnant and wanted to know about me, my medical history, her father's medical history, etc. She said that she did not want to disturb my life but felt the need to know from whence she came. I think she said she had a good family and was not looking for a mommy but was open for a possible friendship. I kept dialing the phone. It was busy.

Time seemed both to speed by and stand still. I went back to the letter. My mother was asking questions.

I said *"Believe me! This is my daughter and I am going to speak to her as soon as the phone is clear."*

"What will you tell your other children?" she asked.

That was very scary, but in an instant I knew my choice had been made long ago. I always said to myself and prayed to God *"If I am looked for, let me be found."*

I dialed the phone again. Busy.

My phone was portable so I was pacing the floor, as is my habit in the middle of any heated, emotional, long or demanding phone conversation. I was wearing circles in the living room. Dial. Busy, dial, busy. I was to learn later this girl could talk on the phone!

So many thoughts swirled around in my head. My other children knew me. They might be mad at me or even ashamed, but they would get over it because they loved me. I told that to myself a hundred times trying to make it true because I knew I had chosen to bring this child into the family no matter what anyone else thought or felt.

I did not want to hurt anyone, but I could not turn my back

on my own flesh. Part of me was almost frozen with terror. What if she did not like me after we met?

Also, there was this joy unspeakable and full of glory I suddenly understood so deeply and clearly. I stood up tall. Straighter. No more secrets weighing me down, keeping me separate from my children and my friends. The chance to be totally free! I dialed again. It was ringing.

"Hello", I said. *"You have found me."*

Cathy yelled to whoever was in the room. *"It's HER".*

2

THE FIRST PHONE CALL

I began to cry at the sound of her voice. Friends and family who have met her have since said that we sound very much alike on the phone. Of course, it was more than the delivery of our words--she has a Pennsylvania twang and I, as result of living so long in Northwest Florida, have a slight southern feel to mine. I found my speech slowing and my words becoming multi-syllabic. But I digress...

She said, *"It's Her."* and we introduced ourselves. Cathy asked about medical things, siblings, her father, her relatives. I recall being calm for awhile, but then I began to cry again when she asked who she looked like and what her nationality was. She said she was going to have a baby in about two months and was really interested in knowing her medical history, if nothing else.

With no reservations, I told her that she was my flesh and blood, and I was, without a doubt, her birth mother. I totally accepted her into my life from the moment I read the opening of her letter and saw the name she was given at birth.

I told her about her brother and sister. She was pleased to know that she had siblings. She wanted to know if they knew about her. I said *"No."*

I asked Cathy to give me a couple of days to tell my son Slade and daughter Sara. Since they were so much younger, I don't know if I ever would have shared the information if Cathy had not found me. The subject is so painful. Not many people want to look the past so closely in the face. Part of me thinks I would have told my daughter, Sara (who was only fourteen at the time) when she got older. Whether I would have or not, I cannot honestly answer.

All I know is that the cave in my chest was full. Joy and extreme gratitude to God for His mercy and loving-kindness filled me. Cat (as she likes to be called) wanted to know the circumstances behind her birth. She said she was not angry with me for giving her up. This it turned out was not entirely true. But I am sure that even she did not know exactly how she felt at the time.

I told Cat about her father, a man I had been in and out of a relationship with during my first two years of college. Our feelings for one another were intense and confused. I wasn't totally honest about him at first. I really did not know what to say, not only because I was concerned how she might take things, but because I had pushed the memory so far down into my subconscious it took a bit of digging to get to the real feelings. I said we were friends who wound up sleeping together one night and I got pregnant. But the truth was we were in love with each other and had hurt each other deeply. Both of us were fearful of being rejected; both of us afraid to say *"I love you."*

My emotions flip-flopped all during the time we were talking. We must have been on the phone an hour and a half after which I was drained and exhausted yet extremely happy. Initially, of course, there was a rush of excitement. I was torn between being extremely ecstatic and utterly terror stricken. Cathy was my daughter--the child that I had given up. She was the child I had set aside and didn't often think about. I didn't allow myself that luxury. I knew I had to go on with my life. I took seriously the giving up of all parental rights, and wouldn't intrude on her or her adoptive parents.

The agency person, who had administered the adoption, assured me that the baby would be given to a special family. I demanded a family that was extremely together, not necessarily financially, but well-educated people who really wanted this baby. I wanted two parents who were going to treat her as well or better than they would their own.

In order to keep my sanity, I suppose, in the interim before our reunion, I never thought of her as *MY BABY* because it hurt too much. I had to let her go, and I did. So, so many tears! So many regrets! Yet there were assurances from everyone that it was for the best. I would think of her around her birthday, and I would say, *"God, if I am ever searched for let me be found,"* then close myself and not think of it again. I didn't think I deserved to be involved in her life in any way and never would have interfered or broken through. But early in the phone conversation with Cathy, *"This was my baby, this was my baby."* echoed in my head. My mind and body regressed.

Remembering actually made me have pain in my abdominal area. Birth pains...I was catapulted back to the hospital room. I don't remember what the rest of the room looked like but my bed was behind a drawn curtain. I could hear the babies crying, but I was the one who did not get mine, except once. The nurse brought her to my bedside and the doctor came to talk to me. I was afraid to touch her for fear I would never be able to do what I knew was the right thing for her. I remember her hair and her beautiful little face. Her hands and feet were so much like both her father's and mine. Thin, with long graceful digits.

Her name was Jane Hilarie after her father John Hilary. She was a finely made, delicate little girl. I recall saying, *"She is so beautiful.* Dr. Milligan said, *"Just like her mother."* He held my hand. I could barely breathe. Then I looked at the nurse and begged her to take Jane away before my courage left. *"Please take* her." So the nurse left with my baby. That was the last I saw of her until the picture in that letter.

Standing in my bathroom to get needed privacy, I looked out the window at the trees in the woods surrounding my house. While this very familiar stranger was asking me questions, I continued to have hard cramps like I was in labor ready to give birth.

At the same time it felt like a coffin had opened and the occupant sat up and said, *"Just kidding, I'm not dead."* The gambit of emotions was difficult to decipher. I felt intense joy because here was the baby I thought was dead to me forever, yet at the same time I felt acute pain and paralyzing fear.

Jane (Cathy) was at the other end of the phone saying, *"I am pregnant. I am going to have a baby in about eight weeks. I wanted and needed to know what was going on medically. I need to know anything you can tell me that I can share with my physician, because I don't know anything about my background."*

As a natural child the answers to the questions she was asking were learned by association and by "belonging." When she asked me *"What nationality am I?"* I began to cry again because it was second nature to me to know my nationality. I tried to imagine what it must have been like for her to grow up without having the information we take for granted.

She said, *"I have a mother and a father. I am not looking for that but I would like to be friends."* That sounded really good to me. I, too, wanted the chance to be friends. Of course, knowing that I was going to be a grandmother was exciting as well.

As I said before, when Cathy asked about her sister and brother I told her *"No, I have never told them."* They had no idea that she was out there. The pain from the past was so intense that I focused on what was positive in the present. But there was no hesitation on my part about wanting to have her in my life. I knew I wanted that long before I received that letter.

As soon as I saw the picture Cat sent, I said to myself, *"You know, there is something very familiar about her face."* I had not even read the whole letter before I turned it over to see if there was a phone number on the bottom. During those moments while I kept dialing and dialing the phone the only thing I could think of was *"Oh, Thank God, Thank God, Thank God, Thank God. It's over. It's over. It's over."* The shame and the humiliation were far outweighed by the chance to get to know my own flesh and blood, my own child. She was 24 years old and I was going to be there for her 25th birthday in November. I was going to be in her life. There was the intensity of grief along with the intensity of joy. My thoughts ran together.

It was an incredible situation. I had to go talk to someone at that point. I just had to go talk to someone. *Systems overload...* I needed to debrief.

3

THE TELLING

I hung up the phone, collected the letter and picture, got in the car and drove across town to see a friend of mine. Cheri, her husband Rick, and three children were home on a furlough from Africa where they were missionaries. I went to see her because I knew that Cheri loved me unconditionally. I needed support to tell my children right away, and I wanted her to be with me and my pastor when I did. Thinking back, this took an enormous amount of trust.

We took a walk. She was staying in this very nice little condo close to Escambia Bay. We sat down along the edge of the water and I handed her the picture. I remember she looked at the picture and then she looked at me. I handed her the letter and before she read the first word she said, *"It's your daughter, isn't it?"*

I said, *"Yes"* and I told her what had happened. She just read the letter and she was there for me. We walked and walked and she allowed me to share my feelings without giving me any advice or making too many comments. She was just my friend, which is exactly what I needed at that point.

I went back to my house but I just could not discuss it with my mother any further. I mean I told her that Cat was her grandchild and I was Cat's mother. Of course my mother was totally shocked because she and my father had been out of the country when Cat was born and I had never told them. My father, who was an aeronautical engineer, had taken a work assignment in Germany, and I felt it was best to not interfere in that plan. They had my sister and brother who were nine and ten years younger than I. I was 21 years old, soon to be 22, and felt that it was something I had to do on my own.

My Dad never knew. He had died three years previously. My mom was there but, to be honest I didn't even think about her. I was so involved with my own feelings about myself and my kids, Sara and Slade and Jenny (my daughter-in-law), that I am afraid my mother had to fend for herself at that point. She was quite shocked and probably quite upset that I hadn't shared it with her, but I just could not really worry about it. I was too absorbed in my own feelings.

After I got through talking to Cheri, I called my pastor. Cheri had promised she would go with me to see him. I was very involved in my church. I felt Pastor Doug needed to know since I had been a member of the church for quite a few years and no one in this little town knew about Cat. I was the singles' leader, my son was in the worship band and most of my friends came from that congregation.

I was close to the pastor and knew he and his wife cared for my family and me very much. He conducted my father's funeral and performed the marriage ceremony for my son and daughter-in-law. My kids had grown up in that church. I needed him to be with me when I told them.

Cheri was with me in the pastor's office. We talked for awhile but I just really didn't know how to tell him. I was feeling such shame. Even after all that time, there was still such shame and sorrow.

Cheri said, *"Just do it the way you told me."* I handed him the picture and the letter. As he read, he just held my hand and was extremely kind. He said he would be happy to meet with the children and me. He said he thought it needed to happen quickly and I agreed.

Cheri said *"Let's go take a picture of you for Cathy."*

At that point, Cathy didn't know what I looked like. She had seen a picture of me as a young person, but she didn't have any idea what I looked like at 46 years of age. Cheri took the Polaroid camera from the pastor's office and snapped three shots. One looked good and I sent it in the mail several days later or one or two days later, I don't know. Time has a way of behaving unconventionally when we are going through this kind of situation. Emotions run high and an hour seems like forty forevers and three days seem like nothing.

I don't remember whether it was one day, or two days, or a week before I saw my pastor with Sara and Slade. All I told them was that I needed them to come with me to talk to Pastor Doug. I have no idea what they thought we were going to talk about. Once again, I was so self-absorbed and concerned about my own feelings I simply was not able to get beyond my raw nerves. I really was worried about how my children would take it. I was afraid to tell my kids, but I knew I must and I knew I would. I was going to have this other child in my life, so there was no question. I would have this baby as well. But there was no doubt that I was scared. I was really scared. I didn't want my children to despise me. I didn't want my children to have to go through additional emotional turmoil. They had been through so much already.

I didn't want Sara and Slade to reject me, but I also knew that I had to be honest with them because I respected them too much not to be. So it was in that meeting that I confessed to an earlier birth of a baby in my life born when I was eighteen. I hadn't even told Cheri until this point.

I could barely breathe when opening up, But, it seemed like

the fair thing to do since I could receive another letter or knock at my door and I could not face trying to explain it. As it was, I made the mistake of not telling Cat and it did backfire on me later.

MY SON IS such a great person who married a wonderful girl and I knew that they deserved the truth. So did my daughter. In the meeting I just told them the same way as I had told Cheri and Pastor Doug. I handed them the picture and had them read the letter. I began to cry. I couldn't stop crying; I was afraid. I was so afraid.

The reaction was decidedly mixed. My son was 20 years old and married to a wonderful girl so he appeared to take the information in stride. My daughter was only 14 and cried profusely but would not talk about it. She closed up like an oyster. She was upset for quite awhile. She did not look at me. I asked her how she was and all she could say was *"I don't know."*

I was especially afraid that my son would be angry with me. I thought he might think I was loose. I don't know what else I thought he might think. My son is precious to me. When I was pregnant with him I would wake up sometimes in the middle of the night screaming because I was afraid *they* were going to take my baby away. Scars run deep. There were some strong feelings about my children that I was afraid to disrupt.

Slade looked at me and said *"Mom, this happened before I was born, I don't think less of you."* He put his arms around me and he just held on to me. I don't know if Jenny said much but she was there for support.

Sara just cried. One strange thing though. As she was growing up she was often talked about wanting a big sister. When she would say that, I would say in the back of my mind. *"Well, you know, you have one."* Sara was such a sweet, special child. I have always been very close to her. She has always been my beloved daughter.

My heart was broken for her. I had to take her mother off the pedestal. And I hated to. She continued to say, *"I don't know,"* when I asked her how she was doing. It took a while, but Sara opened her heart to Cat and now has her big sister.

Once I got over the initial trauma of telling my children, I began to share the news with my closest friends. I was determined that the secret I had lived with all these years was over. I wasn't going live anymore in the shadow of things that had happened twenty-five and thirty years ago. It was akin to Martin Luther King's *"Free at last"*. *Thank God almighty, I'm free at last"* I began to realize that many things in my life had been difficult for me emotionally because of covering up the *sin* of giving up a child for adoption.

As I began to tell my friends, I would watch their faces. Most of them were extremely loving and kind and excited for me. I did have one friend who was rather shocked and basically said *"Well! I guess you just never know about anybody."* But in the end she was very supportive.

Being an *illegitimate parent,* alone through the pregnancy and adoption, had a great deal to do with how I responded to other people in my life. I spent years trying to figure out relationships, bad decisions, and questionable behavior. After Cat found me, I realized that I had an intense amount of guilt. I felt guilty for having given her up. I felt emptiness but never questioned that it was the right thing. I believed that it was best to give her the opportunity to be raised by two people instead of one.

After I knew Cat for five or six years, I changed my opinion. I really am sorry I gave her up for adoption. I wish I had raised her, even alone, as young as I was. Who knows, I may even have gotten together with her father and we might have raised her together. It's unnatural to give up a child, and I would hardly ever recommend it. There was a time when I would have without reservation said, *"It's the best thing,"* but I don't believe it anymore. Perhaps I would not have come to these conclusions had I not had the opportunity to get to know my child.

I know this may sound like sour grapes. But I believe now (as the dictates of society also have changed) that she would have thrived better in the family into which she was born because genetics plays an extremely strong role in the physical realm and in the psychological. Cat would have had much more freedom to develop into her naturally artistic self sooner and probably with less grief.

It wasn't that her adoptive parents were not wonderful. I just believe there would have been a greater understanding somewhere in the *guts* that would have helped Cat find herself sooner. She is still fearful and lacking in self-confidence to the point she has a hard time trusting her own judgment. Neither of my other children seems to have that problem. They have a sense of strength and assuredness. I wish...

There was a spot in my heart that was healing over, but underneath the wound was still there, festering and causing some pain. After speaking to Cathy on the phone a few times, I began to identify what that wound was. It was the tearing away of my baby and the depths of pain and sorrow I never allowed myself to feel beyond that. Even in my marriages I was never really able to give myself to my husband because there was a dead spot in my heart. I don't know how else to describe it. There was a spot that was dead.

The only people I really took into my heart were Sara and Slade. I was unable to let anybody else close. I held back from any person who tried to have a relationship with me. There was too much fear, too much sorrow, and too much certainty of rejection. If I revealed myself, my mate would never be able to accept me so I picked people I was able to love only very superficially so I could reserve a portion of myself.

I knew very little about real love. It wasn't until Cat came into my life with the subsequent birth of Caity about six weeks later, that really began my understanding of unconditional love, along with a sudden understanding of what joy is. I realized that joy is the fullness that comes from opening oneself up and not being afraid any longer. I mean, there was nothing for me to be afraid of anymore.

Suddenly free, I didn't care whether anyone approved or disapproved. I just didn't care. It no longer had anything to do with whether or not they wanted to know me. It had to do with *"This is my child, my flesh, my blood. My daughter returned home like the prodigal son whose father stood in the driveway, looking down the road, waiting, waiting and hoping. Here he comes, here he comes, he's my son whatever he's done, whatever he's been through, he's here. He's here at last, at last."* That is how I felt about my daughter. Cathy was my child. Who cared whether or not anyone approved of the fatted calf being killed? There was only joy.

At last! *My daughter. My daughter. My daughter. My daughter!* I practiced, just as a bride practices the sound of her new name. I wanted to see Cathy, but I also knew that she had a family, and we had a lot of talking to do, a lot of planning to do and a lot of thinking to do. We both knew we would meet, we both knew that we would have a relationship of some type. In those few days it was still like a lump of clay. There were a couple of indentations, but there was no shape yet.

My primary concern over those first few weeks was Sara's reaction to the news. I was watching her very closely and trying to let her know that Cat finding us did not dilute my feelings for her whatsoever and in some ways it just intensified them. I think she was feeling jealous. She was still not talking to me very much, although she was not rejecting me. I think she was deeply wounded and was trying to resolve her feelings. I tried to be there for her without smothering her. I invited her to accompany me to Pennsylvania to see Cat and the baby but she was not ready.

I had so much support from my friends and family members that it was easy to begin making preliminary plans about meeting Cat. The beginning of that summer Sara and I spent a lot of time with Cheri and Rick, who along with several other people in my circle of friends, pooled their money and bought me a plane ticket to go visit Cat in July.

4

A TRIP BACK IN TIME--PREGNANT

It was a gray day in March 1966. I sat looking out of the window, like the past ten days, just staring, not seeing. A few weeks before, back in the small college town where I went to school, I had walked down the street in such a deep funk that I looked up only a second short of mixing with a passing train. I had not heard the whistle at the crossing and almost walked right into the moving cars, the strong wind shaking my body.

I'm pregnant. I know because of the guilt I feel. I want to die. I am angry and ashamed. I don't want anyone to be burdened with me. I picture living with John in a little railroad flat in Lock Haven. I picture him hating me for trapping him. I wanted to go away and never come back. I left school. I withdrew from my classes and went back to another small town, which was my home at the time.

I was staying with a loving family who are like surrogate parents. They had two little blonde haired daughters who I love very much. Kathy, aged seven and Krista, aged four who also love me. How can I do myself in? I lie down for two weeks thinking of dying. Mostly I am thinking of how I could do it without causing grief to the girls. I did not want them to find me and be hurt. I knew they loved me. I thought of hanging, cutting my wrists, taking pills--no way seemed right! I was suffering from clinical depression. The only thoughts that ran together in a straight line had to do with suicide. Not whether or not I should do it, but how and where. But, I couldn't die in front of the girls and mess up their lives with a memory like that.

This day something was stirring me to move. Maybe it was the hint of sun shining just at the edges of the leftover snow, maybe the pale blue gray of the sky, I don't know. But I felt a calling to go outside and for the first time in about two weeks, I got myself dressed and went outside. I remember I was really scared to walk the short distance to the end of the block. Something made me put one foot in front of the other and I was actually walking without feeling the ground, my eyes upward. I was searching the heavens not knowing what for, crying out in my soul for something or someone.

I reached the end of the block and looked down and there it was, a single purple crocus struggling its way through the hard crusted snow, face upward, leaves outstretched to the sun. That single flower was pushing its way up as if to say *"HEY-LIVE"*. I wept and felt alive for the first time in days. I knew it was no accident. I was stirred to see that gentle, tender little fragile flower, which seemed to say *"Everything will be okay."* I looked up at the sky and knew God was watching over me.

I knew God had shaken me out of my chair to see this miracle of His spring, to show me it was not His wish that I die. I must go on doing whatever it was I must do. It was not my time to die. God was very real to me that day and even though it was to be twelve years until I would actually find and accept his wonderful Son, Jesus, God showed himself to me that day on that little street. Today I know that God had me picked out even before I was born.

I'd get through it all. I did not know how. I was so scared and so ashamed. I had so little control when it came to JH. I wanted him, then I rejected him because I hated how much I wanted him. We fought some great fights. Did I love him? I was so bent on sending him away that I refused to even think about it. I was afraid of rejection and so I rejected first. I could bear almost anything but a look in his eye or on his face that showed disapproval or disgust or even faintly questioning his paternity. Telling him about my previous child was out of the question. Had he showed any disdain I would have spontaneously combusted and did on the spot. I chose to walk alone in silence rather than to tell him. The thought of the two of us in a little apartment was frightening. I knew his parents (especially his mother) hated me and any other girl he had ever dated. I really did not know what to do so I ran away and decided to handle it on my own.

The next day I was placed in a hospital that had a floor serving as a mental treatment facility in Ridgway, the town where Cathy was later born. I ate for the first time in ten days. I forgot about God, and made my psychiatrist a poor substitute. I wasn't even really honest with him. I denied my illness and tried to make a good impression on him. I wanted everyone to like me. I cried a lot. I was both relieved and embarrassed to be where I was.

Being suicidal makes those around you nervous, to say the least. I was not officially diagnosed as pregnant so my depression was almost treated by electric shock treatments. That was what they did in those days. Fortunately, my blood work came back positive so I escaped that fate. Pregnant! My heart was shattered. I felt so lost--I did not tell my parents--they were due to go to Germany that summer. My Dad had a job there.

I remember the shuffling feet of one woman who had dyed red hair. She got so violent once in awhile that it took three attendants to hold her down. Then another woman defecated all over herself and two nurses had her in the shower. I was frightened and alone, and at only twenty-one, one of the youngest people in the unit. I was there for a couple of weeks before I was allowed out in the sunshine for a walk with the rest of the inmates with nurses and attendants, of course.

There was a man on the floor (it was a mixed wing with about 25-30 patients), an alcoholic, about 45 who was in there to dry out. We played bumper pool, smoked cigarettes, and drank coffee. We both denied the need to be there. According to us, we were the only sane ones there. (I completely lied to this guy. I told him I went nuts when I found out I couldn't have kids. How's that for a 180 degree turn around?

He had gone to sleep one night and had awakened to find his wife lying beside him, dead. She had passed in her sleep and he was afraid to close his eyes. He used alcohol so he could go to sleep but he would never discuss the incident. When discussing myself with other people, I lied.

There was a young pretty girl, the closest to my age, whose boyfriend (fiancé) had been killed somehow. She was in never-never land. Every day I was there she received an electroshock treatment.

The nurses and orderlies would wheel a little cart around and put electrodes on the patient's head, turn on the electric current and pass it through the brain. Then each was strapped into bed to prevent falling out on the floor after their bodies had been jerked around.

Alternatively they would receive an insulin shock treatment that would give the same results. The floor plan was so open that it was unavoidable to see the treatment. Afterwards the patient woke up in a zombie-like state and was wheeled into the recreation room where orange juice was administered, as they were propped up trying to remember their name, what was happening, where they were, and why.

Thank God I escaped that form of treatment. It seemed

barbaric to me as I watched their heads bob up and down while they tried to re-enter the universe. At the time it seemed less horrible than it does in retrospect. And, today, no one would even consider that form of *treatment.*

Inside the unit I felt helpless and frail, relieved at last to be able to depend on something and someone. My doctor put his arms around me as I cried, as I longed for my daddy to do. I was released from the hospital and came more and more out of my depression. I had a lot of decisions to make as I awaited the birth of my child. Abortion was never an option.

5

GETTING TO KNOW YOU

For the next several months from Mid-April when Cat first contacted me, until mid July when I flew up to Pennsylvania to meet her and Caitlin, we kept in contact regularly by telephone and by letter. We spoke about once a week. Of course our conversations were focused primarily on getting to know each other. What I was like, what she was like, what my family was like. Cat was extremely happy to know that she had a brother and sister and was very anxious to get to know both of them.

Cat's adoptive parents were considerably older than I. They had a daughter who was their natural child, and they wanted to adopt Cat, who was eight years younger than Carol because after Carol was born, they were unable to have any more children. Cat explained that she had been raised in a relatively middle class blue collar/white collar household. Her father was an engineer and worked at a steel company. I don't remember whether he is a college graduate or not. Cat's adopted mother is a college graduate.

I think she grew up in other areas of Pennsylvania as well, but her major upbringing was in Eastern Pennsylvania, in

Lehigh Valley, a small, somewhat isolated area, not too far from Philadelphia and New York City. Bethlehem was light years away in terms of culture, not a bad looking place but it was a steel town populated with a lot of immigrant people particularly from the Eastern European nations.

Cat recalls her childhood as being relatively uneventful. Her adoptive parents took care of her and treated her nicely, but she also talked about never feeling like she fit in. Cat knew from a young age that she was adopted and always felt there was something missing in her life. But she also said it wasn't until she got to be about twenty-two that she actually sat down and told her parents that she really had a strong need to find her natural parents, "especially my birth mother."

Cat said her parents were helpful and gave her what information that they had, which wasn't a whole lot. They were not happy about her quest but they didn't do anything to prevent Cat from finding her natural parents. It took Cat a couple of years to work up the courage. She went from one thing to another until she finally decided to do whatever necessary to find me first. Of course she was also interested in finding her father but always said that her first interest was in finding her mother. She told me she would often look in the mirror and pick out features and then try to see them in the face of other women she passed in a crowd. I related to that as I often looked into the faces of little girls for traces of familiarity.

Cat told me she wasn't angry with me, just grateful that I had not had an abortion and I had given birth to her instead. During our initial conversations she was in the end stages of her pregnancy and was doing pretty well. She was married to a man named Steve. From all the indications she gave me over the phone, Cat seemed happy. Steve's family was from Eastern Europe, Slovak. He was the oldest of three sons. He had been raised in Bethlehem, and his mom and dad still lived there. He was a steelworker. His father had been a steelworker before him and still continued to work there. I really didn't find out a lot about Steve and Cat's relationship until later when I went up to visit after Caity was born. Initially Cat and I centered around what each of us was like, our similarities in personality, what likes we had, what dislikes we had, and that kind of things.

I recall we talked a lot about medical things because Cat was very concerned and wanted to know what to expect about the birth. She knew there were a lot of things that were hereditary about being in labor and having a baby and so forth. I was able to share my experiences with her and the experiences of the other women in the family. It put her mind at ease about her delivery. We come from a family of healthy women who tend to deliver a little bit early and who tend to have short labor. She sounded to me as if she felt reassured by this. There were no serious illnesses or complications that were apparent in any of the family on my side anyway. We talked about my parents and she was interested in knowing about my mother and father and where they came from.

As I said earlier she was very interested in knowing her nationality. I explained to her that my mother was Swedish and German and my father Irish and Dutch. My dad grew up as an orphan because both of his parents died when he was very young. My grandmother on my father's side died in the Spanish flu epidemic of 1918. Throughout my father's whole life he was angry with a God who would leave a child without a mother. His father died from tuberculosis. He had a half sister named Pauline from her father's second marriage and a full sister named Maude who was two years older than him. Both my father and my Aunt Maude had died prior to Cathy coming back into my life so she never would get to meet them.

The more we talked the more excited we became because it seemed we had many similarities in our ways of looking at life and so forth. At least it sounded like that initially, but of course, that is what each of us was accentuating. We were both looking for connections. Cat was looking forward to becoming a mother and was excited about the whole process. I made no plans to go up there at the time of the birth because it did not seem appropriate. I knew her adoptive parents would be there and it just seemed intrusive. But I did want to go visit when the baby was still an infant. As I mentioned before, my friends, who knew how excited I was about everything, actually gave me a shower and bought baby things and a plane ticket.

Although it was very exciting, emotions were very high in my own household and immediate family, as my daughter and my son were coming to terms with having another sibling. My son didn't seem too upset. He was curious but not judgmental. His wife is a very accepting person who had had a very similar thing happen in her family not too many years before. From all indications, the event was not too terribly traumatic to Slade or Jenny. I was later to find out years later that was not necessarily true. The true feelings were hidden.

But my 14-year-old daughter, Sara, was really affected. I remember that summer as one when I spent a lot of time with Sara. We were together frequently with Cheri and her family and other friends who lived on Escambia Bay down the street. I was trying to help Sara understand that nothing with Cathy would in anyway change how I felt about her. My joy at finding Cat was a totally separate thing from my pleasure at having Sara for a daughter and one would not replace the other. We kept communication open between us, and I tried to be there for her as she dealt with her confusion.

Sara exhibited some anger and disappointment but also some excitement. It took her a few years to really get over it. But she tried to be supportive. Since she had always wanted an older sister, she began a relationship with Cat almost from the first week.

Cathy was insatiable for information about us. We spoke at least once a week for two months. It was a very rocky time but I was mostly happy. I was like a kid at a pet store--eyes glued to the little puppy all beige and fluffy. I wanted to meet her and I wanted Sara to come with me to Pennsylvania. Slade was married and in the Air Force so I didn't even think of his coming to meet Cat at this time. He was not free anyway. I invited Sara to come, but she really was not ready to do so yet. She understood that I had to go.

Cat delivered Caity (Caitlin Rose) May twenty-third, 1991. I was finally able to go up to visit her on July 18.

I FLEW UP from Pensacola to ABE (Allentown/Bethlehem/Easton) airport on a Delta flight my friends' had gotten together and paid for. Teresa and Sue and Fran and Sue Two and so many others had chipped in and bought a bunch of baby gifts for me to bring to Cat and Caity. As I made preparations to go to Pennsylvania, my friends kept coming over with words of encouragement and gifts for the baby. Someone gave me a *Grandma's Brag Book* photo album.

Fran came over to supervise what I was taking and what I was wearing. She insisted that I look very *Florida* so I wore this large set of red earrings and a matching necklace, which were of questionable taste to accent a plain off white outfit with a long skirt. I had a really good tan and looked like I lived in a tropical climate. It was out of character for me to seek help dressing but — was a major event and I wanted to put my best foot forward.

Slade and Jenny and Sara took me to the airport and waved me off. They took pictures. I was absolutely beaming and brimming with excitement and anticipation.

Caity was almost two months old when I first saw her. Cat was twenty-four years old, due to be twenty-five in November. In some ways it was like meeting a set of twins. For me both babies were born the same day, July 18.

6

PENNSYLVANIA BOUND

I got on the plane in Pensacola. I was seated next to a pleasant, friendly woman and her daughter. The closer we got to (ABE) the more excited I became until finally I shared with my seat-mate about the reunion with my daughter whom I had not seen since birth. I told her about my granddaughter and everything. It was just a really happy event. There is something about this kind of story that readily draws strangers into it.

We walked off the plane and I stepped out into a little section of the terminal. For a minute I was upset because there wasn't anyone there to meet me. I had visualized Cat and Steve standing there as I disembarked which is how it worked in Pensacola. But there was no one waiting. The first thing that went through my mind was *"Oh my gosh, don't tell me she has changed her mind."*

Then I noticed none of the other passengers were being met either. I didn't know you had to go downstairs. No one was to be seen anywhere. I was not sure what to do. There was a down escalator so I decided to get on it.

In my mind I was saying, *"Well, if she has decided to back out, or is scared or something, I will just call her. I'll tell her I am going to be at the Red Roof Inn for the next four days in case she wants to see me after all"*

I went down the escalator and kept walking until I finally realized that there was only a certain area where people could meet. I just kind of followed along with the crowd and all of a sudden I glanced up. Questions were going through my mind like, *"Would I recognize her?" "Was she going to be there?" "Would she like me?"* Suddenly, I looked up and there she was. I recognized her and I saw her and she was there! The last few steps to her were like running on a cloud. I felt nothing but the need to reach her.

Cat had told me that Steve was going to video-tape us, but the emotion and the anticipation was so great that I didn't even think about it. I remember seeing her, looking at her and thinking how beautiful she was. As she stepped toward me, I dropped my bag and threw my arms around her. I held my child for the first time! I remember saying to her how beautiful I thought she was and she said to me how beautiful I was and in some ways it was like looking in the mirror because her eyes are exactly the same color as mine.

She handed me two white roses. *"Here,"* she said. We just started to talk to each other. The lady from the plane came by. I remember pointing to Cat and saying, *"That's my daughter, that's HER."*

Cat looked at my hands and said, *"Oh, that's where my hands come from!"* I took off my shoes so we could compare toes. She was wearing sandals and we looked at our feet. We just looked at each other like you examine a newborn. We couldn't stop staring at each other and hugged a couple of times. We just had to look at each other as we stood in the airport waiting for my bags to come. I had two with me because most of one whole bag was full of things for her and the baby.

On the way to Cat's place from the airport we stopped at a

restaurant, right next to the Red Roof Inn where I was staying. Because I hadn't eaten on the plane, they both wanted me to have something. I wasn't really hungry but I did eat. It was an icebreaker of sorts. Trying to get to know somebody who looks like you and is a member of your family but who also is actually a total stranger is a mind boggler. I don't know how to explain it other than there is familiarity with the individual yet at the same time you know that you don't know the person.

After we ate, we got back in the car and drove to the house where Steve's mother was watching Caitlin who was almost two months old. It was a very strange kind of situation. Steve's mother was very non-committal and seemed to be pretending this was an everyday experience. She was very odd. It reminded me of the story of the elephant in the living room or the *Emperor's New Clothes*. She was just making believe everything was normal.

Meanwhile, this whole visit was being videotaped. Cat took me into the house and showed me the baby who was still sleeping. This was my first look at my granddaughter and I was trying not to cry. I was not crying externally, but I had all these weird feelings, looking from what for me was one baby to another. We went into the living room to sit down and catch our breath and wait for Caity to wake up. Steve was still taping me as I sat down on the couch and remark how it was like having two babies at once for me.

Cat and I got a lot of laughs later as we watched the tape because in the middle of all this emotion Steve's mother turned to the TV and started to talk about *Hawaii Five-O*. There was never a mention of Cat or me and this unique event. She talked about how one of her relatives visited Hawaii and *Hawaii Five-O* and all about Steve McGarrett and the program.

I looked at Cat and Cat looked at me as Steve continued to videotape. I was thinking, *"Okay, this is Twilight Zone material. Rod Serling is in the kitchen."*

We waited until Caity woke up. She was about two months old at the time. She was a precious, beautiful little girl. We collected Caity and her things, and said goodbye to Steve's parents. The next thing I knew I was in Cat's home. When I walked in, I felt right at home because she and Steve had some of the same furniture I had had when I was about her age. Our tastes were similar, both quite eclectic and interesting.

I began to relax and watch Caity who was a really cute little baby and was easy to fall in love with. When I held Caity the first time my feelings exploded and my heart was full. I kept looking from looking Cat to Caity. Holding Caity I felt so thankful that I was getting a second chance. For me it was also holding a baby from so long ago. I know Cat was fascinated to see me hold Caity. It was quite a full day being in her house.

A friend of Steve's came over to visit and said, *"Wow you guys really look alike."* Everybody kept saying, *" Wow, you really look alike!"* I met quite a few of her friends that first evening and after we had dinner I was ready to go back to my motel. I was exhausted from the emotion of everything and I know Cat was too. We agreed to meet the next day for breakfast.

I was in Bethlehem for four days. I had brought all kinds of pictures with me and we talked about the family. Mostly, I showed pictures of Sara and Slade and Jenny when they were little and how they look now. There were pictures of Slade and Jenny's wedding and my father and mother, aunts and uncles, and my grandparents.

Cat showed me some pictures of herself growing up and pictures of her family, her mother and father and Caryl, her adopted sister. What came through clearly as I looked through her albums was that Cat was *the pretty one* and her sister Caryl was *the smart one.* I felt they were treated according to their roles.

Caryl has a master's degree in social work, which seemed ironic, since I had my bachelor's in the same field. Caryl worked with the mentally retarded and lived in Philadelphia. Cat never finished college. She chose to go to beauty school, and I guess she was a beautician for quite awhile before she developed an allergy to the chemicals and decided to find another career.

The picture started to evolve of a twenty-four-year-old woman with a baby who was without direction in her life. She seemed to be quite happy with the baby and seemed to be taking good care of her. But other aspects of her life were not as they should be. She began to cry one day in her kitchen while she was preparing some food and told me how miserable the marriage was. Steve had gone out somewhere and Cat used the opportunity of his momentary absence to describe to me in detail the kinds of abuse she had been taking from him in their relationship.

I wasn't prepared to handle that information. It was almost too much to take in at the time. Secretly I wished she had not told me. But I was also flattered that she would trust me with this mother-daughter talk. She didn't tell me too much more while I was there, and I did not extend my visit.

I had planned to stay four days, and that was how long I stayed. It was enough for both of us. There was so much emotion and so much we had talked about that we needed time away from each other to sort it all out. I remembered my friend had said she had physical symptoms for weeks after her reunion with her dad and sister even though it was a positive experience. Such a traumatic episode turns your whole world upside down, even if it is good.

I needed to assimilate what I had learned. I saw pictures of Cat when she was little which hurt as much as they helped. They served to accentuate her absence. There were not too many pictures because Cat's adoptive mother was very angry that I was coming to see Cat. I guess she did not think I had the right to see Cat as a baby. She was not willing to share the pictures at this time and Cat was reluctant to make any waves there. I found it to be somewhat understandable.

That was one major difference I found between us. Cat was brought up in an atmosphere of secrecy and *not airing one's dirty laundry in public,* meaning anyone outside the immediate household. She had a lot of fears and was reluctant to do anything without prior approval. In my family we were pretty open, or at least I had always been. When I wanted something, I generally either announced it prior to, or directly after, I did it. I didn't wait for approval or permission. I guess I was given a lot of freedom-maybe too much sometimes.

7

BACK TO RIDGWAY

I stared out the window of the Greyhound bus as I rode from Dubois to Ridgway. It was not a long journey, but the bus stopped at every small town along the way so it took the better part of the morning. I put most of the details of that day out of my mind and had to dig them out which is the hard part of recording all of this. Things you have buried in the deepest recesses of your heart break their boundaries painfully, like pulling off a scab on an open wound. There is bound to be some bleeding even though you know it will eventually heal the wound and allow you to go on without infection.

I think it was spring. At least it seemed warm. I was numb so who really knows? I may go for the records one of these days but not now.

Getting back to *that* day. I maintained control and I am certain that anyone observing me would have made the judgment that I was happy and did not have a care in the world. Internally I was bleeding to death. My heart hurt, my stomach fluttered. Everything was flat lined. I pushed all thoughts and feelings away. I don't remember the room, the clerk, the judge etc.

For me all that existed was a machine making a recording of the words I was required to say. *"I relinquish all rights to..."* beyond that my mind cut off. My guts cried *"No! Impossible! Hell! Anguish!! Cut it off! Stop feeling; it hurts too much."*

It's funny with sad things, how we can sometimes keep feelings inside so closed up that nothing can touch us. I recall telling Cheri on one of our walks that I understood the instant I spoke with Cat why I had such unsuccessful relationships up to that point. I had a dead corner in my heart and her finding me created an additional blood flow that allowed my love to flow more freely. It was as if the finite became infinite. Also, I saw the edge of the enormity of God's love for me to restore a lost part.

Eventually sadness and anger come out in a kind of rage-- seemingly unrelated to the person or situation on which it is dissipated. In my wanderings through life (as I look back now, I can see there was no plan to most of it) stuffing my pain became the most expedient way to get one day to follow the other with a limited amount of trouble. Of course, the day came when rage was so big it had to be expressed. Cat finding me helped me to acknowledge my anger and pain at a system and time that tore mothers and babies apart. There was no welfare or cheese and milk allowance or programs for pregnant women with little or no support system. In fairness to my parents, they probably would have helped but they were scheduled to go to live in Germany and I had no intention of messing that up for them. Besides, I was ashamed to tell them.

There were homes for unmarried pregnant girls whose illegitimate children were seen as temporary and were to be disposed of by giving them up for adoption. In those days even married women were forced to quit work when they began *to show*. There was so much shame and humiliation associated with the unplanned pregnancy. Of course, abortion was illegal and thought of as the guy in the alley with the coat hanger. I am not sure what I would have done if I could have found that *easy* way out. I honestly feel like abortion is the only life affecting decision that gets made hurriedly, in intense shame and at a time when there is no possibility of making a rational choice.

Panic doesn't promote sound thinking. The way a middle class woman in the early sixties handled the fact that she was *used goods* was to hide out in a home for unwed mothers, have the baby, sign it over to *deserving* solid citizens who wanted and could not have a child. Then she would spend a few days recovering, return home, and go on like nothing happened out of the ordinary while she had been out west visiting her *aunt* or whatever cover story her family and best friend put out. From there she was free to bear the pain, shame and guilt all alone. It went swimming around in her heart and belly while she decided whether or not to take the chance of telling the guy she fell in love with, the horrible *secret*. This *standard operating procedure* was not designed for good mental health. It only helped teach suppression of real feelings.

I found out that I was pregnant with Cat after winding up in Elk County Hospital in Ridgway mental health ward for thirty days because I was suicidal. I might describe to you what it felt like to me. When I was in the hospital funny farm of course, I suspected I was pregnant. I did not open up at first because I was ashamed at the thought. It took me a week or so before I would even admit the possibility.

Dr. Milligan ordered a blood test, which came back positive, and he said, *"You're pregnant."* I have a vivid memory of standing in that hospital next to a pool table or something that I had my hands on. I remember throwing my hands up in the air. I did not know what to do. The sheer terror of being single and pregnant in that era is difficult to describe.

I went through the steps of the grieving process. *"No, that couldn't possibly be true, because I only slept with him one night in that particular time frame. I was like hell no, no this can't be happening."*

But I knew it was true because I had all the signs. I was getting sick at my stomach, gaining weight, my breasts were tender, and hadn't had a menstrual cycle in two months. It must have been March or April in beautiful downtown somewhere in Pennsylvania, which is not known for sunny winter days. The day was pretty much gray and damp and cold. I remember that finding out I was pregnant matched what it looked like outside, kind of bleak.

I felt a sense of shame and self-betrayal, because I had slept with JH. Yet, he was someone that I was unable to stay away from. Our relationship was volatile and so passionate that we were as drawn to one another as two people can be, yet both of us were proud and had explosive natures. We tended to fight and fight, then make love and fight again. Although we did a lot of things together, and enjoyed the same things, our relationship was extremely passionate and intense.

Even after I found out that I was pregnant I didn't tell him. He found out from someone else. I didn't want him to feel obligated to marry me. I wanted him to marry me because he loved me. Years later, I found out from JH that he had come to the hospital and wanted to ask me to marry him. I vaguely remember his being there, and he described our meeting as very awful for him. *"I felt so rejected," he said. "There was a pool table and I kept trying to get close to you and you kept running away. We would up circling the table a few times before I gave up and left."*

I was drugged at the time on a couple of different medications, which really affected my ability to make any kind of decision. I repressed our conversation. What happened between us was very sad because we each felt rejected and unwanted by the other.

I sent JH away. I came to my senses a few weeks later after my head cleared and I was released from the mental ward. Then

I called his house and tried to see him. I was rebuked and thought he didn't want me. That we walked away from each other lends incredible sadness to the whole situation because we are, in fact, well suited. I was heartbroken.

After I got out of the hospital I had to have some kind of plan that would allow me to continue my counseling. Dr. Milligan treated me like I was one of his troubled children. He was a Catholic with seven children and incredibly kind to me as he helped me face the reality of my situation. I needed him and his support so much. The initial plan after I got out of the hospital was that I would continue to see him on an outpatient basis. Where I lived was about a two-hour drive from Ridgway and I didn't have a car. I think I went down to see him a few times.

The next few months are a fog except that Ruth, the social worker from the adoption agency in Ridgway, talked me into going to a Florence Crittendon Home for unwed mothers in Pittsburgh. Whether someone drove me there or I took a bus, I really don't remember. I arrived at the home for unwed mothers and was unprepared for the setting. I hated it from the moment that I arrived until the moment of my departure. I was in college. I stayed there for about two weeks, which would have made it some time in July. There were only one or two of the girls that I even wanted to share my private agony with. It was very upsetting to me.

I remember feeling like part of a freak show because anywhere we went all the big bellies together announced our shame. Most of the girls were in classes to complete their high school diplomas. They must have been a lot younger than I, except for one woman who was my age and also a college student. Carol and I became confidants. She was not due until late September or October and I was due November first. I thought we could help each other through the ordeal. I needed someone to talk to especially if I could not see Dr. Milligan. I was still quite fragile emotionally.

But Carol went into labor, and had the baby prematurely about the 13th day that I was there. Usually once a girl had the baby she was gone without so much as a goodbye. I remember the rumor was that the baby was very little, maybe less than four pounds. I just saw Carol for a brief moment after the birth. She was crying. She said *"Don't wish for this to happen to you. Don't pray for it to be over too soon."* then she was whisked away.

I was despondent and cried for the next few days. I could not stay there; there was no one for me to talk with. The people at the Crittendon Home finally called up Ruth, the social worker in Ridgway, and told her that staying there was not the best for me. I also told her she was going to have to get me out of there so I would be able see Dr. Milligan to continue with my treatment.

Ruth called up her pastor, Father Brown, to ask if there was anyone in the congregation willing to house me until I gave birth. The Episcopalian church where she attended was filled with influential people. Ruth either came to Pittsburgh to get me or met me at the bus in Ridgway.

My emotional state reflected the trauma I felt, so memories are sparse in spots. I do vividly remember Father Brown and his interview with me.

Ruth had told him the whole story including my previous pregnancy. He needed to know but promised it would be confidential, although I felt harsh judgment from him. It was humiliating but Father Brown had spoken to a couple in his congregation who were willing to let me stay in their home until the baby was born. He did chastise me for my unfortunate state and admonished me to act like a decent human being. I don't think he warned me not to steal the silverware, but I sure felt like a criminal.

I spent that night in Ruth's home, which I now know was an

unusual thing for a social worker to allow. The next day I was taken to meet Bob and Loretta Miller. They were very wealthy and had a beautiful home set on lovely property on a very nice street in Ridgway. I guess it was one of the nicest sections in Ridgway, but I wasn't paying a lot of attention at that time. I was just grateful to have a roof over my head.

Bob and Loretta were wonderful to me and treated me with dignity. Their kindness helped me make it through. I settled in, and I had this little room and my own private bath. I pretty much had the run of the lovely house. I can't remember how many bedrooms it had, but they picked it because they wanted a large family. Bob was retired by then, Loretta was in her mid to late forties, and their dream for a child never happened.

After being there a few days it happened to be my birthday. Bob and Loretta were leaders in the community of Ridgway, so when they took me in, their friends also welcomed me and treated me very nicely. In fact, they brought birthday presents and Loretta had a cake for me. I was very touched by the party and began to relax.

One of their friends loaned me some maternity clothes. Bob and Loretta took special care to invite a few people my age that I spent a lot of time with while I was in Ridgway. I was treated kindly as a decent person who was in trouble. These folks life-style resembled my background and education. They were intelligent and educated. I understood where they were coming from and did not take advantage of anything. We played bridge, and I did a few paintings as well as some of the cooking. The neighbors were great; it was much more in line of what I needed than the unwed mother's home. Most importantly I was able to go to my regular counseling sessions with Dr. Milligan.

I was in Ridgway throughout August, September, October and a portion of November. Bob and Loretta were really concerned and visited me in the hospital after the baby was born. That was certainly a big help since it was one of the hardest times in my life. The greatest help came from Dr. Milligan, whom I saw two or three times a week at the end. My relationship with him was the most important thing that kept me going, even with Bob and Loretta being so kind.

It was obvious to me that Loretta wanted the baby. It also became very obvious that Loretta could not take care of a baby as she was an alcoholic. Bob drank a lot also, but Loretta would often be drunk by five PM She would hug me saying, *"You are just like the daughter I never had."* Sometimes it was more than I could bear. I hated for Loretta to be sad about not having children, but I was not going to let her have this one.

Fortunately, I was able to escape to my room when they had people come in almost daily for cocktails. There was one particular bright spot when a woman named Mildred came to stay with Bob and Loretta, just shortly after I got there. Unfortunately for Mildred, she was there because her husband became too ill to travel back to their home. He remained in the hospital for about two months before he died so, I never did meet Frank. Mildred stayed on for the funeral and burial. I recall hugging her and telling her I was sorry.

Mildred was an extremely colorful person. She was a Southerner, from Mississippi and was a very different breed from any of the people in this small town in Pennsylvania. She was genteel in many ways and definitely the *"Grande Dame."* She talked to me like a friend about the baby and the baby's father and was genuinely concerned for my well being.

Although she was party to the cocktails every night, Mildred did not get sloppy drunk like Loretta. It was a good diversion having her at the house, as Loretta was able to give her attentions to Mildred as well as myself. There was card playing several times a week. Bob and Loretta belonged to a bridge club, and had a special card room. Fortunately, I knew how to play bridge and often joined in as a fourth. In that household there was a great deal of entertaining all the time.

It was obvious the Millers were members of the elite in Ridgway. As such, they received lot of invitations to really nice parties, and I also got to go to some of them. People were always being invited over to the house and there was always good food. I wanted for nothing. I grew very fond of both Bob and Loretta.

In light of the situation I couldn't have asked for a better place. The only exception, which gave me mixed feelings, was my determination that Loretta was not going to have my baby. Fortunately, because I had the backing of Dr. Milligan and Ruth, I knew that this would not be a threat.

What strikes me as odd is that I remember Doctor Milligan and our conversation and how comforting he was, but I don't even remember my medical doctor's name. I do remember one small encounter in his office that was excruciatingly painful and embarrassing for me because his nurse keep asking me *"What's your husband's name?"* in front of a room full of woman with ears perked up to listen. As I have said before, this was the sixties in *Small Town USA* and to be pregnant out of wedlock was a big deal. I was somewhat speechless. I think I finally got out, *"I have no husband."*

I just don't remember that doctor examining me. I don't remember his face, his voice, or questions he asked of me on any of the visits. I woke up early on the day of the labor and delivery. That morning I sat on the toilet and discovered that my water had broken. I remember going to the hospital but not how I got there. It was not a long delivery. Next, I was in my room, and the baby was brought in. I don't remember the medical doctor ever coming in.

At that point I recall a nun that talked to me very briefly, as I cried she asked, *"Did you expect it to be any different?"* Not very comforting, I must admit. There was one bright spot socially, a couple around my age, Michael and Lee, whom I particularly liked and with whom I had a lot in common, remained my friends even after my pregnancy. I would walk over to visit Lee and sometimes she and Michael would come over to visit Bob and Loretta. They had a child; a little boy named Chris, who was really cute. They were educated and intelligent and really helped me to pass the time. While I was in the hospital Lee stopped by and gave me a gift, which was a touch of kindness I really needed.

8

WILL THE REAL ME PLEASE STAND UP?

Before I became pregnant I thought a lot about God. But *A Supreme Being* was more a concept and not a big part of the equation. I kept my life segmented and I was constantly involved in a struggle to find out the real me. I wanted to be like someone else, instead of being the *ME* that God intended.

Living in a small town afforded me many opportunities. I was in a local beauty contest one time sponsored by the area Jaycees. I lived a clean, wholesome life in one town—spent time with all the right people of wealth and good reputation--I was invited to the right parties, and dated the most eligible bachelors. But when I went to college in another small town three hours away, I satisfied the more Bohemian side of my personality by running with an outcast bunch.

Part of me was *Miss Sorority*, the other part, when off campus, belonged to an artist colony. I lived in a constant state of duality, internally frantic as I looked for *right and wrong*. I was always searching for the meaning of life. When in conversation with many of my sorority sisters, I got the feeling that my questions made them feel uncomfortable, like they could not understand what I was talking about. I found out later that it was because of who I am. I tend to make some people uncomfortable because I look straight at things and dissect them. It took awhile to accept that part of myself.

Most of my sorority sisters had a clear idea of what they were going to do with their lives and did not have this driving urge to search beneath the surface. At least that is what they said. My other group of friends, the artists, would talk for hours on the *meaning of life* in such depth that it would always seem they returned to the same spot. *"Do your own thing because no one knows what they are doing anyway."*

In some twisted way, the artists may have been closer to the truth than they imagined. After all, they were the group that accepted individual taste, choice, and even responsibility. The sorority types seemed contented with the *status quo.*

Most of my friends in that art colony were avowed atheists. Yet, it is amusing to note that we spent a great deal of time discussing a *Supreme Being.* This *Being* was credited in some way as responsible for the dilemma in which we all seemed to find ourselves.

Always looking for the truth, I spent a lot of time alone. Saturday mornings were my favorite alone times. I would dress in warm clothes in the dead of winter and walk the mile and a half into town to a little restaurant for breakfast. I loved it-alone with my thoughts strolling along the river on a crisp, cold morning while the snow was falling. Yet, somehow, somewhere, inside, I was searching for God. I would rise at seven o'clock Sunday morning and walk to the Catholic Church for a service. Afterward I would go back to the dorm and out to the art gallery to foul mouths, loose actions and non-caring attitudes.

I played a different game when I went home for weekends. I was one of the *"Belles of the Ball"* in that small Pennsylvania town. I had dates-one Friday, one Saturday, one Sunday afternoon. Sometimes I had two dates in the same day, all different guys, and different types. I avoided involvement. As soon as a guy seemed interested, I began moving away. Besides, I knew if these people found out about the *Real Me* it would be all over anyway.

But I could not seem to shake this one guy at school. JH was a *Townie* who hung out at the art gallery. I was fascinated by him. He was tall, handsome, and intelligent, with a great sense of humor. He was also a little odd. Ours was a real tumultuous relationship, since we both had strong personalities. I loved him very much but would not admit it. We had many battles along with our good times and he became the father of my baby. We eventually succeeded in hurting one another very deeply.

As I look back on that period of my life, I realize I was looking for the thing that all humans search for--love and acceptance. But because I did not accept myself, no one could break through the protective barrier I had around me. I was unable to accept love, indeed even to recognize it. JH tried hard enough.

Barbara, my roommate from the last two terms had decided not to room with me so we no longer had the apartment on Main Street over the opera. A whole bunch of pilots moved in and I don't know why but it just did not work out between Barbara and me for some reason. We decided not to stay there together, so I was alone in this new place. I can't even remember if she was in school that term or not. She may not have been.

I had this dreary little room off campus right over the rail-road track. I remember old-fashioned yellowed wallpaper and bad smells. The shotgun style made it kind of narrow and dark and there was ugly, worn linoleum on the floor. It was cold and noisy, all in all, not an enjoyable home. The only thing to recommend it was the close proximity to the school.

I was having a particularly difficult time at school. I was tired and burned out, as it was my sixth term in a row with no break. I wanted to see the one person I knew would be happy to see me. I was feeling very lonely. I walked about two miles in the cold to get to JH's house. He was at home, alone and the stage was set. JH's parents were on vacation in Florida, an irony not lost on either of us when we later met again in Florida.

I had not seen JH for awhile because so much was going on. It took me a couple of rum and cokes to get my courage up. It had been a typically dreary February day in central Pennsylvania, which added to my mood and my need for companionship. Once at JH's, we talked, drank a little wine and shared an intimate night, which was to change the course of all our lives forever. It was not premeditated but predictable. It took almost thirty years to get back to him and work out the situation.

JH was someone I had known for a long time. I adored him and couldn't stand him at the same time. I was so upset and distraught over a number of other things that I didn't even know how to gauge the relationship at the time. It was strange. I felt a deep amount of love I did not know how to show, so I treated him shabbily and rejected him mightily. In the end the tables turned.

To make a long story short, I decided the best thing I could possibly do for the baby was to give her a chance at a normal family situation. I knew that between the two of us, as volatile as we both were, it would probably be better to give our child a firm foundation. As it turns out later, I can't think of a decision I have regretted any more than that particular one.

There haven't been too many other choices that have impacted me more. I did deeply love this man and found out later, he also loved me. It was a tragedy all the way around, yet we all survived it seems. I can't tell you the degree of sadness I still feel because the depth of despair is measured individually.

I knew I couldn't make this child suffer for my foolishness. I couldn't recognize that I was really reaching out for love and that I really loved JH. Like I said before, it was a love-hate thing. He was so attractive to me that I couldn't keep my hands off him. I had this desire for him like I have never had for anyone else. I found out later, *Hey, that's normal!* but I grew up in the fifties and sixties before the sexual revolution.

Women weren't supposed to have *those* feelings until five minutes after the wedding. You were supposed to have the marriage ceremony, eat the cake, have a champagne toast, and all of a sudden turn into a love goddess. Only then were you supposed to have sexual feelings. You weren't supposed to have sex on your mind prior to the wedding; at least that is how we were brought up.

Turns out he is the love of my life.

I graduated high school in 1962 and to be a woman who was on fire with desire for this guy made me into some kind of a freak in my mind. I was scared of him and scared of the whole thing. I did everything I could to discourage him. I know I confused him because it was a push-pull. *"Oh let's make love, never mind don't touch me, leave me alone, and come back."* When we met years later we spent a lot of time talking and unraveled the bizarre thinking. In our own feeble immature way, had we tried back then and had some kind of a clue what to do, we may have made it work.

There was always that intellectual pull. Like I was in his head and he was in mine. There are regrets after making mistakes and poor decisions. Sometimes you get a chance to make up for them or redo them, but most of the time that doesn't happen. The reality is there is a lot of life in between.

But, I will always love him.

9

CAT COMES TO FLORIDA

I t was mid-January when Cathy stepped into the reception area at the Pensacola Airport looking a lot like a little girl holding baby Caitlin. Caity was about seven months old and as cute as could be. It was Sara's first face-to-face meeting with Cat and Caitlin and a very emotional moment for a mother to see her two daughters together for the first time. Slade took a picture of the four of us together that I entitled *The Girls.*

Slade and Jenny met us downstairs at the baggage pick up. The first thing that Slade said was, *"My God, Mom, she has your eyes! They're just like yours; it's really freaky."* We all laughed and joked about whatever people do under those emotional circumstances. My mother was there also.

Steve had bought Cat the ticket to come to see us in Florida as a Christmas gift. I was really excited because I had told everyone I knew about her, and of course I wanted her to come to meet Sara, Slade and Jenny, my mother and other family members who lived in the area. I wasn't very sure how everybody would feel about her since my child was new to them. I just wanted for Cat to come and meet the people who had sent her all the baby gifts and had together bought my plane ticket so that I could go visit her in Pennsylvania.

One of the highlights of the visit for me was having Cathy and Caitlin in church with Sara and me on the day my son Slade was singing a special song. My heart was full, and I was so thankful for the mercy of God. It was one of those *It doesn't get any better that this!* moments. My family and my best friends, just basking in His love, surrounded me. People kept coming by to greet Cathy and Caitlin and hug me. I think we videotaped part of it.

That Sunday afternoon after church, I held an open house with a buffet and invited about fifty of my friends, relatives and closest co-workers. My intention was to legitimize Cathy by introducing her to people that I knew. I felt that I was taking my child out of the closet. I wanted to honor her; I wanted to give her a place in my life.

Cat sat in a chair as people passed by her. My guests made comments like *"You sure couldn't deny her, she looks just like you." "We are so happy to see you reunited with your mother." The more I see you, the more you remind me of Bonnie."* My friends embraced Cat and they passed Caity around. They were extremely kind to them; but then my friends are very loving and generally very accepting.

Part of the reason I wanted her to meet everyone was so she could get some idea of who I was by the company I kept. I also wanted her to be able to put faces on the ones who had sent her baby gifts. That afternoon is one I will always treasure. I am sure it was awkward and overwhelming for Cat but she handled it very well and seemed pleased that I would do that for her.

This visit lasted about ten days. Cat and Caity used the room downstairs that used to be Slade's so she would have a chance to get off alone if she needed. It was a major event for Cat as she

THE CIRCLE IS COMPLETE

was dropping right in the middle of all our lives and meeting a
lot of new people.

My son John had not yet reunited with us at this time.

We explored the region, going to Pensacola Beach, the
historic downtown area, Fort Pickens and a lot of other *touristy*
places, as well as to friends' homes, and businesses and meeting
relatives for meals. One day we drove to Destin, about seventy
miles away because I wanted to show her one of the most beautiful beaches in the world. I will never forget the expression on
her face when she saw deep blue water for the first time. Destin
is a part of the Gulf Beaches known as *The Redneck Riviera*.

The trip had been her Christmas present from her husband
Steve, who I think was in the "I'm sorry and I'll never do it
again" part of the cycle of domestic abuse known as *the honeymoon*, which usually followed a violent episode. Cat shared how
fearful she felt when he threatened her and opened up to me
quite a lot as we spent time together hanging out. When Steve
did call it was obvious that there was not a lot of warm affection
between the two. I believe that he became verbally violent over
the telephone.

Cat's obvious problems put somewhat of a damper on the
visit and my enjoyment of the relationship. But, again, I
accepted her as my child, my daughter who needed help. My
background in social work and history of working with
battered women made it impossible not to worry about her
safety when she went back to Pennsylvania.

I advised Cat to think through what she wanted to do and to
be very careful. I was even concerned about her going back into
that situation but she indicated that she had to because she had
to decide what she wanted to do and resolve her conflict. I
knew the marriage had problems because after my Pennsylvania
visit Cat called about once a week and talked with me sometimes for hours at a time. It was my intention to keep our dialog
open, so I allowed her to call collect and most times she did. We

talked about our relationship, the baby, her marriage, and almost all things in between. Her adoptive parents were having some problems dealing with our reunion, especially her mother, Rosemarie, who felt threatened by Cat's interest in me.

Apparently her marriage was getting worse again and she was quite fearful and did not know what she wanted to do. Bob and Rosemarie did not have experience with an abuser or abusive relationships so they were not able to help Cathy as much as I am sure they wanted to. Because of my professional experience and in that in my own personal life, I was able to point out some of the power and control issues and help her to make a safety plan. I had been briefly married to a man that never actually hit me, but he was definitely an abuser.

I knew Steve and Cat's relationship was going bad. Because of my background I got sucked right into wanting to rescue her. I had just found her and did not want to lose her, so I became very protective. When I went back to work, I sent money and kept writing to her. I regularly sent things to Caity and Cat so that she would feel that she had somewhere to go if she wanted or needed it. I tried to help her realize that there was someone that really cared. I can see now that I went too far initially, probably in part because I felt guilty that I had not been there to mother her while she was growing up. I was going to do so now, no matter what.

On the plus side was a chance to be with my granddaughter. My mother and I took care of Caity for the day when Sara, Cat, Slade and Jenny all drove to New Orleans, three–four hours away. We had a great time playing with Caitlin. She was a happy baby, alert and lively. We got to know each other a little bit and that was wonderful fun. I was thrilled to be a grandmother and felt I was blessed with a second chance with my daughter.

The ten days at my home cemented the relationship between Cat and Caity, Sara and me. Cat had also had a chance to get to know her brother and spend a little time with him and Jenny, and my mother. She and Caity had met my brother, his wife and an aunt and uncle. There was definitely a family feeling between all of us, and they were accepted into the fold. No matter how difficult or award some moments were, overall the visit was wonderful.

Holding baby Caity

Caity - Halloween 1993

Being a grandma is fun!

Three of my four children

Cat, striking a pose.

Caity

Caity on a visit.

Family

Having fun

10

CAT GOES HOME

After her visit with us, Cat went back to Pennsylvania and her abusive marriage. While Cat was with us, she decided she had to make some serious decisions to insure her safety and sanity. I believe Rosemarie and Bob were at the airport to pick up Cat and Caity, not Cat's husband Steve. Cat opened up to her family about the escalation of the domestic abuse she was suffering. Since they had no experience with anything like Steve's behavior, it was difficult for them to understand the danger Cat was in. Cat had felt ashamed of Steve's behavior, so she minimized the details of his intimidation, emotional, and physical abuse.

But like many abused women, Cat returned to her home and shaky marriage. Cat wanted Caity to have the benefit of a father in her life. Cat still had hopes for the relationship. She also had no way to support herself at the time. Steve continued his verbal abuse and became more violent, drinking heavily at times and even brandishing a gun.

During that time, Cat called me frequently and we had long conversations regarding Steve's behavior, his cycles of violence and remorse, and what she needed to do to insure the safety of herself and the baby. As with most victims of domestic violence, Cat felt there were large barriers to living on her own, such as lack of money, dependence on Steve for medical insurance, etc.

Cat always tells me that my support and understanding of the dynamics of domestic violence helped her to be strong. A few months later she was finally able to move out to her own place and leave Steve without being seriously hurt. Of course, Rosemarie and Bob were there for her also, with practical advice and financial support. They were very concerned for the safety and well being of Cat and Caity. She actually had the best of both worlds.

At the same time Cat also started having a series of illnesses. Initially her doctors diagnosed her ills as psychosomatic due to her emotional state. There was no doubt her emotional problems were contributing to her health problems, but Cat also had some severe allergic reactions to foods and medications causing her to go the emergency room several times. Cat went from one physician to another, visited an allergist, and even saw a psychotherapist. Despite her best efforts, she got very little relief from her symptoms.

Over the next year or year and a half, Cat developed serious mental and physical problems. Obsessed with her health and getting no satisfaction from physicians, Cat developed an odd eating disorder symptomatic of Obsessive–Compulsive Behavior. She was not bulimic or anorexic but she was only comfortable eating a limited number of foods. I believe that she only ate five different things, mostly rice and ground beef. At one point she had her own skillet, and a dishcloth and sponge that she used exclusively on her dishes. These symptoms were outward manifestations of her inward need to control her fate, her destiny.

Concerned for her health, as I was for my other children, I remember suggesting that she continue her counseling and do something about officially ending her marriage. She remained married to Steve several years after their separation. She did have her own apartment, but it was not too far from where she and Steve had lived together. Since Cat chose to remain in Bethlehem, a very small town, there wasn't really any security. No matter where she went, he always found her.

From my understanding he did not initially bother her much by going to her new apartment or harassing her on the phone. Once she did go outside in the middle of a snowstorm to find her tires slashed. She felt certain it was the work of Steve or one of his drinking buddies. This kept her scared and off balance.

I remember she called me one time because the police had made her leave her apartment after Steve went to a local bar waving a gun and making threats to *"Get the bitch."* The police confiscated the gun and arrested him. Cat stayed away from her home for a few days and finally secured a restraining order after that. For a while the police did ride by her apartment to monitor Steve's activity.

Even though I warned Cat about getting involved with anyone too quickly, she was too afraid for her safety to be alone. She started spending time with a friend of Steve's, who like Steve, was about fifteen years Cat's senior. Like many battered women she was so concerned about being protected, she did not have much energy left to make decisions. She was blown away and needed someone to lean on. His name was Tom. Cat sent me some pictures of him and Caity, but I never actually met him. Tom was quite supportive of Cat and helped her to start standing on her own two feet again. Cat worked hard to get her health back, to care for Caity and to start over in a new and better life. She had been traumatized by Steve's abuse and was suffering from low self-esteem along with her other problems. She kept blaming herself for making a bad choice and reached out to me because I knew better. Like many abusers, Steve quickly got a new girlfriend who shared his passion for alcohol and left Cat alone. He showed no interest in Caity.

I tried to be understanding and supportive during the next several years as Cat integrated our reunion with all her other experiences into her new life. No doubt her changes topped the stress chart, as did mine.

Sara stopped over in Bethlehem for a few days to be with Cat and Caity during a trip that Sara had taken to visit her grandparents in eastern Maryland. Sara wanted to visit for a few days because the two had begun a sister relationship during Cat's visit to Pensacola and had shared many phone calls, cards and letters in the year that followed. Sara met Cat's other sister Caryl and the four of them, including Caity spent a day in Philadelphia, where Caryl lived. Sara had fallen in love with Caity and was delighted to spend some time with her.

It was also during this period that Cat and Sara drove from Bethlehem to Wilmington, Delaware, to see Ann and Harry Helmstadter, the couple I lived with while I was in college. It was their two daughters, Kathy and Krista who had played a large part in preventing me from carrying out my thoughts of suicide. It was also Ann who gave Cat my phone number and address when she was searching for me.

Ann and Harry had been a big part of my life for many years and were among the very few people that knew that I was pregnant with Cat. They were like second parents and I remained close to Ann until her death in 1997, and still keep in contact with Harry and their two daughters. They were with me for the births of both Slade and Sara. In fact, the night I delivered Slade, I began having labor pains at Kathy's twelfth birthday party. She was having a slumber party, and all the kids stayed awake for news from the hospital. My son was born shortly after one in the morning.

When Sara was born, I lived only about two miles away from Ann and Harry and the girls. My pregnancy was a difficult one and as my husband traveled a lot, Harry took me to the hospital on more than one occasion. The Helmstadters were very supportive, and I knew they loved my family. When Cat found me they were excited and happy for me and wanted to meet Cat and Caity.

Tom drove Cat, Sara and Caity to spend the day with Ann, Harry and Kathy. Krista was not there because she lived out west with her husband and two sons. It was a great reunion for Ann and Harry and Kathy who had not seen Sara since she was about three years old. Of course, they had never met Cat even though all those years they knew of my longing for her. They were thrilled to get to meet Caity who was about a year old by then.

11

_____

DIGGING IN

The relationship between Cat and Sara was solidifying, because as I mentioned earlier, Sara had always wanted a big sister. Now she had one. Sara claims that somewhere down deep inside she knew about Cat. Slade and Jenny also stopped by at Cat's place to see her and Caitlin when they were in Pennsylvania for Slade's grandparents' fiftieth anniversary party. My children accepted Cat as part of the family, in such a matter of fact way that it really made me count my blessings. There seemed to be no jealousy on their parts at all.

Cat continued feeling ill with little explanation or relief from her illnesses. She was still eating a diet lacking in proper nutrients and continued to suffer from allergic reactions. Her counselor apparently quit. Even though at that time she sought out alternative medical treatment, she remained fearful of trying new foods and did so only at the office of her allergist, who was armed with epinephrine in case she reacted negatively. Everywhere Cat went, she carried a bag containing a needle filled with epinephrine.

Cat and Tom had stopped seeing each other. Now, in our

conversations over the phone I began hearing about a guy named David who was also known as Dano. He was a local musician and guitar player and repairer. They had been friends for quite a long time. Eventually, they almost moved in with each other. Caity was quite fond of Dano and became attached to him. Cat and Dano were together as a couple for about two years and have remained friends.

We met Dano when Sara and I flew up to Bethlehem in late October to celebrate both Sara's birthday, October 15th, and Cat's, November 1st. Caity was two years old at the time and a real cutie. We spent five days with them that fall. We all went to the mountains to see the fall foliage, and we had a beautiful walk with Caity, who was running and playing with the leaves.

The more time we spent with Cat the more I understood the differences in our values and belief systems. This of course, I did not initially notice. As with all reunions, there is a time when the honeymoon is over. Cat and I began to tiptoe around each other a little less, so to speak. It is inevitable in all relationships that the time comes when you have to evaluate whether or not the price you pay for that relationship is too high.

Cat had many problems, and she was obviously looking for someone else to solve them for her. I just happened to be the next one in line, or so it seemed to me. After finding me and putting a face and name to her mother she once again was disappointed because I was not a magical solution. I think Cat expected that once she found her natural parents, everything would be all right because she thought being adopted was at the root of all her problems.

I became really concerned for her welfare because I could see that she was having severe emotional distress. She needed some serious counseling, but that didn't seem to be forthcoming.

Symptomatic of Cat's emotional state was hypochondria, poor eating habits and other symptoms of Obsessive-Compulsive Disorder (OCD). She seemed to be so absorbed with herself and her own illnesses that I began to wonder about her ability to be a mother to her baby. Not that I thought she would do anything deliberately to hurt or neglect Caity, I just wondered how much attention Cat was able to give a child given her own emotional state. Of course, anytime I tried to broach that subject, or suggest some help in that area she was offended. My motivation was to help, but I think Cat thought I was being critical of her parenting.

It became apparent that any relationship, even one that is welcomed, has its pro's and con's. I wanted Cat and Caity in my life. I was happy that she found me. I totally took Cat on as my child; she was 100 per cent my daughter to me. The advice I gave her was what I would have given to Sara if she had been in the same position. In my mind there was no difference, and I felt Cat needed reality, not platitudes. I saw she was in trouble and wanted to reach out a helping hand. When someone asked *"How many children do you have?"* I would always say three. (John was not in the picture yet.

I forgot that Cat didn't know me like Sara and Slade did and didn't understand how I operated. We lacked the years of history that make up a mother-daughter relationship. Often we spoke of the sense of confusion that we both felt. Cat related stories about how she would be talking with someone and say something about *"her mom in Florida"* and *"her mom in Pennsylvania."* People would get confused so she told them the story of our reunion and dissolve into tears.

My experiences were similar. I would tell the story about how she found me and it was very emotionally charged, even two years later. I wanted her in my life, but I also realized that she was, at least temporarily, a person who was extremely needy. I knew it was going to take a lot of my time and effort to develop our relationship into a healthy one.

I can only compare it to the commitment one makes to a

BONNIE L. QUICK

newborn, since that was what she was to me, at least emotionally. When you bring a baby home from the hospital, you have midnight feedings, you have to change the diapers, and you have to hold the child, as well as take care of sickness. I found that being reunited with my adult child also triggered those nurturing behaviors because of my need to make the initial bonding happen.

The reunions on television are reminiscent of the joy of looking into your newborn's face the first time your child is brought to you and laid on your stomach. When you bring that infant home, the first few days are ecstasy. Your friends surround you and congratulate you and coo and cluck around the precious little thing. You are excited and delighted in this wonderful miracle. Hopefully, that wonderfulness never goes away when you think about your children.

From day one, you bottle feed or breast feed them; you choose their clothing; you take them to the doctor for their first shots; you do all of the other things that you do with your infant. You record their first steps and first words. But somewhere in time this infant represents inconvenience. There are times that you do not feel like getting up at 2:00 in the morning to feed the baby or change that diaper. You don't want to listen to that baby cry and may not feel like giving them their dinner right now, but you do it because it is part of being a parent,

What I found in my relationship with Cat is that the same principle applies. She was, in a sense, a baby. I treated her as if she were emotionally my newborn. That dynamic happened even though neither one was conscious of it. I listened for her cry and I wanted to feed her, if not a physical feeding then an emotional feeding. I wanted her to look to me almost as the baby in the crib would and reach out to me and know that I was going to be there.

As I look back, I can see that I took her on emotionally as I would an infant even though she was a grown-up. Other

72

members of my family could see that she was grown up but I did not see her that way. She was my baby, my infant, my little daughter, and I saw her as the little daughter that had been returned to me. She was a beautiful daughter that looked a lot like me. Some things reminded me of her father who was long limbed and good-looking. She had his smile and dry wit. I also had a nice little baby, my Caity, who was a bonus. It was like seeing Cat as a baby, wonderful, and very pleasant, but, at the same time, it was also very demanding.

There is a need to make a connection, which of course, is not as easily done with an adult as with a baby. We tried to bridge the gap of time by talking and looking at pictures and comparing taste in clothing or music. We talked about everything from religion to politics, grandparents to sisters. She would show me something and I would say " *Hey, that reminds me of me when I was your age.*" Or she would see a photo of me, and say *"I see myself in that one."*

At that point, we were filling in a frame, putting flesh on a skeleton. We were building the sculpture around an armature, picking up little pieces of clay, one after another. Each day we built upon on our knowledge about each other. As the three dimensional image emerged, it was incredible how easy it was to identify which parts hereditary and environment had played in influencing her tastes and viewpoints.

I sensed fear, anguish, and uncertainty in her life that I think she was blaming on having been an adopted child. As is true in most situations, not everything is necessarily traceable to one event. I don't like everything that Cat does and no doubt she feels the same about me, but that doesn't change our biological and emotional bond. I told Cat repeatedly that she was totally accepted by me. Cat became more certain of her place in my life. As she relaxed Cat began to feel free to disagree with me and free to tell me how angry she was feeling toward me.

12

CAT'S FIRST FAMILY

I think as Cat got emotionally free to feel anger at the circumstances of her life she expressed it to everyone as she attempted to put all of us into perspective.

To protect herself, Cat had learned to stuff her negative feelings inside herself and tended to blame her fate on being adopted.

According to Cat, she was raised in an environment that did not allow free expression of feelings because her feelings were not understood. She said she was not able to express herself very well.

She would not voice her feelings outright. She could not say, *"I am angry with you", "You really make me mad"* or *"I like this, but I don't like that".*

Cat spoke in the past or future. *"I was going to do this, or I am going to do that, "* while she was stuck in behavior patterns that were counter-productive.

I don't mean to imply that she wasn't trying to get everything in order. She was pulled between two loyalties because she was adopted. Part of the adoption mystique and language said if you love your adoptive family you will be satisfied and won't need to know your birth parents.

For a while Cat felt guilty and was secretive when she called or wanted to come see me. This aspect of the complicated relationships between all of us is almost to be expected. No one knew each other. She was very concerned that she was going to hurt Rosemarie and Bob or me.

I found it difficult because although I never wanted to hurt Rosemarie and Bob either, I knew there was probably no way to avoid that. Adoptive parents tend to believe, not necessarily at a conscious level, that they have to compete with the birth family. Perhaps it really does require a hierarchy of relationships.

FROM MY POINT OF VIEW, Cat was 25 years old and had sought me out and found me. I did not weasel my way in. I felt it was time for Rosemarie and Bob, who had her for all her life to feel secure enough in their relationship with Cat, to allow her to get to know me and stop throwing up roadblocks. I was not trying to steal their daughter. I was very respectful of their feelings, willing to meet them and ready to answer their questions. But they still were not ready to meet me.

I had gotten very tired of having to pussy-foot around Rosemarie and Bob's feelings. We were a couple of years into this relationship, and I thought by now we would have come to an understanding. Caity was my grandchild as well and I wanted to be able to see my grandchild, talk to my grandchild, and exercise all privileges of the relationship as well as deal with what seemed to be mostly the down side of Cat's life.

Cat often called me for advice on *"What should I do about this? What do you think about that? I am going to do so-and-so."*

I would try to present options, but my advice would not usually be taken. It seemed that Cat's *modus operandi* was to call, talk for hours, take advice from me then call Rosemarie and Bob and get their advice. Since we came from almost opposite ends of the spectrum on most things, it only confused the situation. Then she would talk to someone else, thus diffusing her anxiety, and enabling her to move too rapidly toward solutions. It was very confusing for me for a while.

When I finally realized that she was just testing me to see if I would be there, using me like a teddy bear to comfort her, I felt some anger, I am not sure why. Maybe I was hurt she did not take my advice. I was tired of having to continuously consider everyone else's feelings when it seemed that mine were ignored.

What seemed lost on Cat was that our reunion was as difficult for me as for her. I had not invaded anyone's life nor had I gone anywhere that I was not invited. I was really tired of feeling pitted one against the other. The dynamic was similar to what children of divorce do between estranged parents. Much of this may have been due to the confusion that Cat felt because of trying to integrate and pick from two totally different philosophies.

I am somebody who tends to have a straightforward style of communication. I don't feel comfortable beating around the bush and according to Cat Rosemarie's style is the direct opposite. But, I had never met Rosemarie so I had only Cat's input. I am sure it became hard for Cat to juggle all the different factions.

On the other hand I think Cat thoroughly enjoyed all the attention as she attempted to integrate her upbringing with her natural self. I think most anyone in her position would have felt the same.

I wanted to do it all perfectly. I wanted to go back and start over. I couldn't make up for the time we were apart, but I wanted to. I couldn't make up for making a decision based on what I thought was best for her, but again I wanted to. I lived with extreme guilt for a long time and wanted to make it up to her.

I needed to be her mother, and, at the same time, I knew I

wasn't going to be the mother who would be there for Christmas or Thanksgiving or Easter or her birthday.

It was a bit of a gamble, and I felt very weary because I wondered just how did she fit into my life and how did I fit into hers.

13

BIRTHDAY

Cat's twenty-fifth birthday was the first birthday I celebrated openly with her. I went to the store to buy her a card.

Buying her a birthday card was a perfectly natural event, yet at the same time monumental. I went to several stores to find the right birthday card. I definitely wanted to get a *Daughter* card, but initially I couldn't find one that was suitable because most of the cards were either too juvenile or else filled with remembrances I did not have.

I was getting a birthday card for my child, a person I barely know that looks like my family while I have no memories of feeding her or changing her diapers. It feels a little amnesiac.

I wasn't there to hold her up when she rode her first bicycle. I wasn't there when she skinned her knee or went to school for the first time. I wasn't there when she got her first tooth or when she lost her first tooth. Santa Claus, the Tooth Fairy, and the Easter Bunny all belong to another time.

I wasn't there for any of those things that make someone a parent. Yet at the same time when I sit across the table from her

I see my eyes or hands and her father's smile and her father's hair. And I feel the sting.

As I read through the cards one after another, each one seemed less appropriate than the other.

The *"Dear Daughter"* cards would say you are grown up now, but I remember when you were little. The text mentioned how you bruised yourself when you fell off the bike, or your first day at school, or when you went to your first dance. Another bunch spoke of the pride in how much you have grown and even though you are not a little girl, I am still your Mom kind of thing. Internally, I was bleeding.

I was standing in the store and I began to weep, the tears running down my cheeks, while trying to find this card. I realized that it was the most important thing in the world for me at this particular moment to find that perfect card.

When, finally there it was, a card that said *"Happy Birthday! You are my daughter and I love you."*

That was all I wanted to say. So, I grabbed the card and paid for it and quickly got out of there. People were walking up and down the aisles and I am sure someone saw me crying in the store.

I have since written an all occasion card that says *"You may not have always been in my life, but you were always in my heart."*

The grief and thankfulness meshed into an emotional sweet and sour soup. The year after Cat found me was full of mixed emotions, the emotion of regret and guilt and sadness and the emotion of elation and joy and happiness were all intertwined.

Since then we have been lucky enough to share numerous birthdays but I will never forget that day.

14

CAT VISITS FOR THE SUMMER

W hen Caity was about four years old, she and Cat came to Northwest Florida to stay with Sara for about six weeks. The first week or so of their visit I was in Melbourne, Florida, working. They got to spend their time with Sara and Slade and Jenny. Cat had ridden down from Bethlehem with two of her friends who were able to stay only a few days before they drove back home. Sara had moved into her own apartment for a while, wanting, at age 18, to be independent.

Sara drove Cat and Caity the five hundred miles south to Lakeland to give them a chance to meet my sister, her husband, and children and to see my mother again. I finished up my two-week stint and drove over from Melbourne to meet them for the weekend. I then drove Cat and Caity back to my house, since Sara had to leave earlier to get back to her job.

We had a good family reunion. Cat met my sister's family and Caity enjoyed the pool and the kids. Cat had worked up the courage to call her birth father again to see if he would be willing to meet her while she was so close to his home. Although he had spoken several times with Cat, it took him four years to be ready. He agreed. It was quite an experience for all of us. This episode will be discussed in the next chapter. Cat, Caity, my nephew Adem and I left a few days later and drove back to Milton. We were just ahead of a tropical storm that was brewing in the Gulf.

It was summer (July and August), in the panhandle. It was hot and humid enough to be a steam bath and also it was the height of hurricane season. I mention this because Cat was petrified of storms so she was uncomfortable with our raging lightening and thunder so common in Northwest Florida.

Cat and Caity did not like the woods experience either. They were definitely city girls. We had lived in the Florida woods for years and were familiar with the flora and fauna. The house was up on stilts as are most like homes near the water. We were about two acres from Blackwater Bay and across the street from an estuary. When Caity walked outside, it was obvious she was afraid. Cat was also afraid of the snakes and the bugs, both of which are plentiful in the area. Cat was bitten by a brown recluse spider, something that none of us had experienced in the thirteen years we lived in the house. The spider's venom can cause scarring if not treated properly and is very painful.

During Cat's stay, Hurricane Erin came through the area. Cat and Caity went to Sara's place because it was on higher ground and farther away from the water. I stayed in my house in the woods until it made sense to evacuate to insure my safety. I went to stay with a close friend in town so I could easily return to check on my animals. The roads were only open to residents in the area because of water and downed electric wires, so I didn't see the kids for a few days. We kept in contact by phone.

While Erin caused no significant damage to the property, a few trees came down and we were without electricity and water for almost a week. But, like true Floridians, we dried off, cleaned up, put on the air conditioner and continued to move forward. I had accepted a transfer to Melbourne, Florida, and had taken off a month to get the house ready to rent. The debris from the storm added to already large pile of sorting and packing I needed to do.

Our trips to surrounding beaches more than made up for the *little inconveniences* we suffered at Erin's hand. Cat, Caity, Sara and I spent a lot of time in the sun and surf relaxing and having a great time just enjoying each other's company. Cat and Caity also spent quite a few nights with Sara in her apartment across the bay in Pensacola in a more populated and concrete world.

Cat had come with very little money and without trans-portation. I loaned her my car a few times while she was in town. Cat came into the house one day after being at the beach saying, *"Mom, I wrecked the car."* Actually, what she did was run into someone's trailer hitch and put a fair size hole in the bumper. I could only laugh because it was something I had missed from her as a teenager. In the scheme of things, a hole in the bumper was a minor problem to me.

My fifty-first birthday was truly one of the best of my life. The year before my landmark fiftieth birthday, my mother and my friends gave me a surprise party. That was wonderful, but this one topped it. All three of my children, my daughter-in-law and my granddaughter shared a birthday dinner with me at an Italian restaurant. I had presents and everything. You could not imagine how much we laughed. It was a hilarious evening. I felt so good, so fulfilled. My three children were at my birthday for the first time in my life. Just remembering it makes me teary-eyed.

There is no comparison between four days and six weeks. Six weeks allowed us all to move into a deeper relationship. Sara and Cat got pretty close. We were forced to be more real with each other and hopefully everyone relaxed more. Cat is very intense and does not easily relax in my presence. That temperament trait comes to her naturally. I struggled for years to learn how to take life less seriously. Now I have decided to enjoy each day as it comes. I spent a lot of time playing with Caity and was happy to have the opportunity of seeing my grandchild grow up.

One example of the fun we had was the day Sara and I put bananas in our mouths and ran around the house making chimp noises to amuse Caity. Cat just stared at us. I don't think she had ever seen anything like that at home. Sara and I have always had a lot of fun together and can act crazy.

When Cat was ready to go home, Sara and I took her and Caity to the Greyhound station where I bought both Cat and Caity bus tickets to Nashville where they were going to catch up with a friend of Cat's who would drive them back to Pennsylvania. So, I really got to play Mom at long last. Sara and I cried because we knew we would miss Cat and Caity and planned to see them again soon.

15

JOHN (JH)

At various times during those first years Cat and I were seeing each other it was natural that questions about her father would come into the picture. I told her the facts that I knew about him, erroneously reported in information she had from the adoption papers. But when she pressed, I usually answered *"You know, I haven't seen him in a long time."* I really didn't have much to say about her father because in my mind he was dead. After we walked away from each other, I had the baby, gave her up, and only saw JH one more time after that. Though we spent a few hours together, we barely discussed her. Neither of us seemed to be able to face the issue. So, figuratively speaking, I killed him.

When Cat asked me questions I really could not answer them, and I did not want to answer them, either. It was very painful for me to think about JH and that period of my life. I was doing some OPS contract work for the State of Florida's Health and Rehabilitative Services (HRS).I remember sitting at my desk and suddenly breaking into deep, intense sobs. I was embarrassed but I could not stop crying. I don't know how long this was after I first spoke to Cat. It was only a few days, I would

84

guess. Few people knew. I sobbed non-stop for about an hour. I was a social worker who had a private office so I closed the door and just let *"er"* rip. I confessed to several of my co-workers who looked at me wide-eyed.

There were telephone books from all over Florida at the HRS office to assist people to find *"deadbeat"* Dads who were not paying child support, among other things. I had made a call to a friend I went to school with who had also known JH and asked if she had any idea where he was. She said she thought he lived somewhere in Florida. I started with the A's and soon I had the city where he lived, his address and his telephone number. It took less than fifteen minutes to locate him. Prior to that moment I had no idea we resided in the same state.

Actually, my brother telephoned his house for me because I really did not want to create any problems for him or his family. My brother introduced himself and only told John that I needed to talk with him. When JH called back, I told him that Cat had found me, she had a baby, and I had made the decision to include them in my life. By then I had already told my children, family and close friends.

"I knew it was either a life or death announcement," he said.

We had a lengthy telephone conversation, which was initially somewhat awkward and formal, since we hadn't spoken in over twenty-five years. At first I was near tears and he remarked on the shakiness of my voice. That seemed to bother him a great deal. He asked me about my family and what I had done with myself. His questions were pointed. Things like, *"How is her eyesight?"* and *"Does she have the same speech patterns as you?"* and *"What does she look like?"* I didn't know until later that some of his questions were a result of doubts he had about his paternity. He had never confronted me with those doubts before.

What he said on the phone that night was that he felt he would like to be involved but wanted to see me and talk with me before he met her. I made arrangements to see him a weekend when I went to my mother's house. But, he did not call back to set the time. I felt that he had to come to terms with this event in his own good time. Besides, JH said he had never told his wife, and that had to be done before anything else. They also had a young daughter to consider.

I knew that JH would eventually get in contact or be open for contact from Cat. It was for him to decide whether he wanted to meet her and how he wanted to handle her in his life. His timing was going to have to be his own and that is exactly what happened. It took another four years before he was ready to make the initial meeting with Cat.

Not meeting JH was very distressful to Cat at times. Although she would say that she was very happy that she had gotten to meet me, and glad we were becoming friends, she was getting more and more curious about her father. I had not told her about my conversation with him, especially since he did not follow up for our meeting. I wanted him to have a chance to assimilate the idea and make his own decision. I didn't want Cat to jump to any conclusions. I had sent him pictures of Cat and Caity after my trip to Pennsylvania. My motivation was to protect Cat from feeling rejected. I know now that was an impossible task.

Eventually, I finally admitted to her that shortly after she found me, I called him. She said she understood why I didn't tell her right away. A couple of years later she called and cried and said she had been upset all Father's Day and wanted to meet JH. I told her that if it bothered her that much she had every right to call him and tell him. Cat was planning on a visit with us for the summer. It would be possible for us to make a trip south to meet him part-way between the two towns.

We spent about two hours getting ready to meet JH. Cat was a nervous wreck and changed her clothes a couple of times. I had mixed feelings about going with Cat to talk to him. I suppose I was a little curious, but after he had stood me up, so to speak, four years earlier, I wasn't really all that excited. I guess I thought it was possible he might change his mind again. I don't know. My original plan was to watch Caity, who was four years old, while JH and Cat met to talk about whatever it is he would talk about to a daughter who was 28 years old and had never met him before. It would be their first real father-to-daughter conversation.

As it turned out when Cat called him, he said that I needed to be there at the meeting and intimated it might not take place otherwise. I left it up to Cat. She decided that she needed my moral support. Off we went to the local Holiday Inn. It was not a very busy place, which is why I picked it. We wanted to have time to talk without being pushed out in a hurry.

The last thing Cat asked me before we walked into the restaurant was *"Do you have any 'shoulda, coulda, wouldas?'"* I had never heard that expression before but I knew what she meant. I said *"No."*

There was only one table occupied by a lone man. It was JH, but what a different man from the one I remembered from twenty-eight years ago! The last time I saw him was probably about six months after Cat was born and, although, we talked, it was obvious that he was angry and otherwise occupied.

Thirty years ago JH's hair was dark, the kind of hair that is not all one color, like Cat's, thick, with lots of body. Now his hair is that silver color, which makes him look much softer somehow. His eyes are blue, yet all these years I had pictured them brown. Strange how the memory changes things.

After the Holiday Inn closed, all of us went to find another place we could continue talking. At Denny's we shared a piece of coconut cream pie and about three o'clock in the morning in Denny's parking lot, Cat took pictures of us. It was the first time we had ever been photographed together. Cat said *"This is like being on Mommy and Daddy's first date."*

I hugged him and wanted to hold on until the past melted

away. He hugged me back with the same fervor. Then he hugged Cat. What a great moment! I can still see him watching us as we drove away, standing beside his white Audi with a contented grin and a look of wonder on his face. The only comparison I find for that experience was in the hospital after the birth of my other children when *Daddy* looked into the face of his new baby with pride and approval. It was very healing.

16

CAT'S THOUGHTS

Note: I asked Cat to write this chapter to give her the opportunity to say how the reunion felt to her. This is the letter she sent me as it was written.
From Cat:

I COULDN'T TELL you when I was told I was adopted. I always seemed to know. Growing up wasn't much different from the *"natural child's"* experience. I had an older sister and parents with a solid loving marriage.

Somewhere along the line, I decided to locate my birth mother. This was a definite *"maybe I want to do this"* in my mind. Over the years I had asked my folks numerous questions about my circumstances. They were very honest and forthcoming, sharing any and all things I requested. I had the natural desire to see a face resembling mine. Ask any adoptee. We share this common feeling of being disconnected. *Medical history. possible siblings, heritage, and who's nose do I have?* were the things that plagued me the most.

In the late 80's I started a half-hearted search with the information I possessed. I joined a self-help support group for adoptees, birthparents and anyone touched by the triangle of adoption. Adoption Forum helped me (not to search) find the courage to face my fears. Fears of intrusion on some-one's life, rejection and failure to locate her.

My mother was threatened by my urges so I did not share many thoughts or feelings with her. I felt somewhat guilty, like I was betraying her so I periodically would break away from my search as clues unfolded.

When I was twenty-four years old and discovered that my husband and I were expecting a child, instead of feeling pure joy, I felt terror. Terror about the unknown medical history. My obstetrician asked me to fill out the standard *"family history"* and I explained I had no clue due to being adopted. He suggested undergoing tests including an amniocentesis later in the pregnancy to rule out birth defects and/or possible compli-cations.

That was the moment I made the decision, no matter what, to do everything in my power to locate my birth mother and family. My baby's health was more important to me than stepping on toes in my (adoptive) family. I had no money to spare for a private investigator or to register my name in the *Soundex* organization (a worldwide network of birthparents and adoptees trying to find a match.)

Three cheers to Adoption Forum. In our monthly meetings we shared how to utilize information sheets. Non-identifying information (NII) sheets provide brief physical and educational descriptions of parents with no names or locations disclosed. Amended birth certificates, social and adoption agencies, and even the presiding judge's name can give a clue.

I was extremely fortunate. I had two very important clues. The first was an NII sheet. There was a paragraph labeled *"mother"* which said *"Aged 22, blue eyes, brown hair, 5'5" 120 lbs, completed two years of college and plans to continue education."* Second, I had a court document changing my name from Jane Hilarie xxxxxx to Cathy Ann XXXXXXX. With these small pieces of information I pieced together an idea that perhaps my mother had continued to go to college in Pennsylvania (where I was born).

I was attending Penn State Allentown at the time, and went to the library and paged through the yearbooks looking for women with the last name Church. When I opened the 1969 book to the *"C"* section, I saw a lovely young woman--B.L. Church, who I couldn't deny resembled me closely.

I still get chills thinking about that moment because I knew in my heart I had found her. However, being the skeptic I am, I didn't want to pursue this person based only on that information. I rang up huge long distance phone bills calling every court, every person listed on documents and the agency.

Finally I had another break. After calling a lady friend of the social worker (now deceased) who counseled my mother, I was instructed to call the hospital where I was born and ask for a specific person who I will keep anonymous. This beautiful woman obtained (against the law) my birth record and told me my mother's birth name was Bonnie Lynn Church. Now I knew B.L. Church and my mother were one in the same!

At this point, I am about four months pregnant and I had a tremendous sense of urgency to find her. I assumed she had married and changed her name. So I hate to admit it but I told a few lies to the Pennsylvania University Alumni Association to obtain her last known address. Turns out it was from 1971 in care of someone named Harry Helmstadter, Jr. Thank heavens it wasn't someone named John Smith. Ma Bell of PA provided me with two Helmstadters in the state, neither matching the address I had.

I called Mr. Helmstadter, Sr. who had been a councilman from McKeesport, and he said *"Yes, my son and his wife know Bonnie, call them in Delaware."* I was so close to the end of my journey.

I waited days to make the call. I was so afraid I had my friend call for me under the pretense of a *"genealogical family tree study"* or some other BS. I got an address for Bonnie Quick in Florida. I never in my life, before or since, felt such trepidation. I composed a letter, which was very formal and I included my photograph and phone number.

I was seven months pregnant when I got the call from Bonnie. It was a beautiful positive experience. Nothing can express the joy I felt two months later being able to call her minutes after I had given birth to her perfect Granddaughter, Caitlin Rose.

I thought *"What a great ending."* But, it was the beginning. Almost eight years later after many letters, laughs, tears, fights, and phone calls, I know I have found myself and the circle is complete.

JOHN, CAT AND I

.

The three-way reunion added a totally new dimension to the mix. I did not expect to have the kind or intensity of emotional response that I had following the meeting. When Cat told me JH had said, *"Bonnie has no choice but to come to the meeting."* His arrogance issued a challenge to me. I assumed any residual feelings I might have had for him were long dead. I went only because Cat was very nervous and said she needed me by her side.

I was surprised how difficult it was to leave JH after that night we met with Cat. The sound of his voice and the smile on his face said there was something unfinished between us. Later, I stared at the pictures of the happy people Cat had captured on film, especially the one of JH and me with our arms around each other, beaming with joy.

My thoughts ran wild. *"Dare I ask if there is a chance for us NOW? I know for certain that I cannot think of never seeing you again."* A tragic event had left me fragmented. Meeting JH again brought a sense of completeness back to me. For the first time in my life I felt like I was not alone with my grief. Until that night I did not know I needed John's support, but suddenly it became important. It had been magical to look from Cat to JH and see the similarities between them.

I was divorced and JH was separated from his wife, but still married. He had a daughter in high school that was living at home. I knew I wanted JH and me to be in one another's lives in some capacity and he said he wanted the same. We agreed to meet each other a few weeks later after Cat and Caity went back to Pennsylvania. We both needed to bring some closure to the past and a positive direction to the future.

I brought photos of Cat and my other children. JH brought some of his daughter and of himself as a child. We sat mesmerized looking at pieces of each other's lives. There was a resemblance between his other daughter and Cat. I could tell that something in Caity's pictures also reminded JH of his girl. I recall him putting his finger up to the bridge of his nose and stroking it gently to note the resemblance.

We went to an Italian place to eat. I will never forget the pasta we shared over my tears. Over dinner JH asked me a few questions he did not want to ask in front of Cat. The answers explained to both of us how we had managed to misunderstand each other. I felt embarrassed at my public display of emotion. He kept saying I had cried enough over the years and that he wanted to make me feel better.

After that weekend, I finally grieved for the loss of JH, for our baby, for the death of our relationship, and for the fear and misunderstanding that came between us. As Monty Python said while standing on one leg, bleeding in the midst of the carnage, waiting for the knight on horseback to make his next move —*"IT'S A MERE FLESH WOUND."* Thirty years of life had passed, yet it was as fresh as today.

JH and I visited Cat a few months later. We rented a van and drove to Pennsylvania for her twenty-ninth birthday! I had called Cat and told her what we wanted to do. I asked her if it would be okay. She agreed and said she was both excited and petrified. It was twenty-hour drive so it meant a relatively short stay and a quick turn around to drive back but it was worth it to us. Our child was to have both her natural parents with her on her birthday for the first time in her life. We were creating a major memory entitled *Birth Mom and Bio Dad --The Birthday*. So where was Oprah when you needed her?

When I went to Pennsylvania the first time I was willing to meet Bob and Rosemarie and talk with them. As it turned out it was probably best that we didn't because it was emotionally charged enough for Cat and me to be with the baby and Steve and Cat's friends. JH would not be meeting them this time either. It was just too much for *his* first trip and too much for Cat to have all four of us together.

Before the trip, I was eating lunch at an outside table in front of a little Cafe owned by a Frenchman. It was a delightfully sunny fall day. I was very excited at the thought of our upcoming trip. Observing a father with his infant daughter sitting at the next table, I fantasized about what JH would have been like with Cat as a baby. He would have wanted to call her Katerina! I guess that would have been okay with me, as it sounds Russian and I always liked the Russian name Natasha.

The young father held his baby tenderly. His eyes were wide and amazement was still on his face. It was not unlike the look JH had when he first saw Cat. I imagined him in the hospital room taking her into his arms and coming to the side of the bed to give me a kiss. I felt sad and yet somehow, complete, with that photo in my mind.

There were several days of *Gosh; it's good to be here!* moments while we were in Bethlehem. Playing with Caity, eating in that German restaurant, having a drink and talking in that little neighborhood pub, going out with Cat and her friends to hear her boyfriend sing. Driving around in the van laughing about John's *"dead reckoning ability"* as we searched for street signs and the entrance to the airport was fun.

Although I had celebrated Cat's birthday with her before, this was JH's first one. I was glad to be there to watch her open the gifts JH had selected. She cried when he handed her a Teddy Bear to make up for the one he never gave her before. Next, he gave her a collection of his favorite books. The books were perfect. He even had one for me. *"The Hitchhiker's Guide to the Galaxy."* (I had absolutely loved listening to it on tape during the drive up.)

JH also met four-year-old Caity for the first time on this trip. She was playful and friendly. JH has a gift for relating to young children and Caity opened up to him. He was cute with our granddaughter, talking and teasing with her. I nearly cried when he read *"Good Night Moon"* to her. She got up next to him and just cuddled. When we left, she said *"Good Night, Grandpa John."* He looked a little misty.

We both felt concern for the well being of Cat and Caity. We wanted to show Cat that she had our acceptance. JH especially had a willingness to be there for her and Caity. He wanted to reach out a hand and see her get out of the mess she was in. We both were sad that Cat and her husband divorced, leaving her a single Mom.

I had been to Bethlehem twice before so it was probably an easier trip for me than for JH. He wanted to give Cat a chance to go to college. He offered to help her financially if she wanted to go. She was twenty-four and seemed to be headed nowhere fast. Cat chose not to take him up on his offer and he felt rejected by her refusal.

From JH's point of view, the two of us had come up together to see Cat at considerable effort. He felt we had opened ourselves to her, offering what he saw as an opportunity for a wake up call. JH wanted to see Cat make the effort to go to school so she could have a better life for herself and her child. He was very disappointed that Cat seemed to want to get ahead without making an investment of time and energy. I thought there were some entitlement issues from Cat. I don't know first hand what her expectations were. I do know she was experiencing emotional problems that probably interfered with her ability to understand what she was turning down and how it would adversely impact her life.

I found it interesting that Cat is a photographer and she never took a single picture of John and I together during the whole visit. There was no picture of JH, Caity and I either the whole five days we were there. For that matter, no record was made of the three of us together except for a picture taken by a staff photographer at a local paper. I never understood why that happened. There was one shot of JH reading to Caity and that was all.

Over the next three years, JH and I continued to see each other from time to time. Cat did not seem happy that JH and I were in contact. She may have been angry because of JH's choice not to take as active a role in her life as me. She may have been jealous of the relationship between JH and me. I know Cat was hurt and it did interfere with the relationship between her and me. I felt Cat forgot that the impact of the reunion was as great on both JH and me as it was on her. We needed to find closure also.

18

A NEW PERSPECTIVE

I remember hearing a sermon a few years ago in which the pastor explained how the word *sincere* developed. It is a Latin-based word, coming from two root words, *sin*, which means without and *cere* which means wax. So, *sin cere* means, without wax. During Roman times, walls were built using large quantities of bonding material to cement the rocks together. It was the practice of some unscrupulous contractors to use the less expensive wax as a filler ingredient in the cement mixture. The wax melted when the sun came out. The weakened walls fell apart and structures collapsed. From the outside, the construction looked sound, but it was internally compromised. Wax was a cheaper building material that did not perform as needed. So, it became common practice in Roman times to include as part of the contractual agreement a promise that the materials used were *sin cere*, without wax, and therefore had the structural integrity necessary to hold up the wall. *Sin cere* evolved in common usage to mean *true--without anything false*. After I heard that sermon, I realized anew how important it was to build a sincere relationship between Cat, Caity and me.

It must be *without wax*, free of filler material that could melt and run off and cause it fall apart.

Any healthy relationship needs to be built on a solid foundation of trust. The truth needs to be told no matter how painful that might seem to either side. To say, "You   or "You are really ...   or siblings involv   s another mothe

When I beg four or five yea rift Cat and I h *The Letter* becar book "The Circle wrote her to reco my life despite wanted Cat to kr received her first l in time when she h

From day one I   The consequences of th   and not matter enough to keep me from her. That subconscious decision had been made long ago. "*If my child found me, I wanted her in my life.*" Since our reunion, I have talked to many other birth parents and adopted children who have made other decisions.

The responses run the gambit. *"I don't want to see this child because nobody knows about it "* to *"Yes, I would like to get with him. I have never had any other children and would welcome a relationship."* Several people expressed fear that the child would not be what they wanted them to be. *" I know she is going to be thirty- five and has a right to know her mother but I am afraid if I find her she won't be Jewish or Catholic or whatever. What if she is this or that? I can't face that so..."* The number of excuses and explanations is infinite.

In order to get to know your child you must be prepared to

pg 100

first sentence:

- - -

could melt (?) run off and cause it to fall apart.

A NEW PERSPECTIVE

I remember hearing a sermon a few years ago in which the pastor explained how the word *sincere* developed. It is a Latin-based word, coming from two root words, *sin*, which means without and *cere* which means wax. So, *sin cere* means, without wax. During Roman times, walls were built using large quantities of bonding material to cement the rocks together. It was the practice of some unscrupulous contractors to use the less expensive wax as a filler ingredient in the cement mixture. The wax melted when the sun came out. The weakened walls fell apart and structures collapsed. From the outside, the construction looked sound, but it was internally compromised. Wax was a cheaper building material that did not perform as needed. So, it became common practice in Roman times to include as part of the contractual agreement a promise that the materials used were *sin cere*, without wax, and therefore had the structural integrity necessary to hold up the wall. *Sin cere* evolved in common usage to mean *true--without anything false*. After I heard that sermon, I realized anew how important it was to build a sincere relationship between Cat, Caity and me.

It must be *without wax*, free of filler material that could melt and run off and cause it fall apart.

Any healthy relationship needs to be built on a solid foundation of trust. The truth needs to be told no matter how painful that might seem to either side. To say, *"You are really my child"* or *"You are really my mother,"* doesn't negate the other parents or siblings involved. *Birth Mom* is not a replacement mother. She is another mother.

When I began to write *The Letter, A Birth Mother's Journey,* four or five years ago, it was motivated by my desire to mend a rift Cat and I had. Starting out as a Christmas present to her, *The Letter* became the first chapter of this work, the current book *"The Circle is Complete—An Adoption and Reunion Story."* I wrote her to reconfirm my happiness about her involvement in my life despite our disagreement on an important issue. I wanted Cat to know exactly what my feelings were the day I received her first letter. I wanted to share with her that moment in time when she had found me, her birth mother.

From day one I was ready for Cat to come into my life. The consequences of that choice did not matter enough to keep me from her. That subconscious decision had been made long ago. *"If my child found me, I wanted her in my life."* Since our reunion, I have talked to many other birth parents and adopted children who have made other decisions.

The responses run the gambit. *"I don't want to see this child because nobody knows about it "* to *"Yes, I would like to get with him. I have never had any other children and would welcome a relationship."* Several people expressed fear that the child would not be what they wanted them to be. *" I know she is going to be thirty- five and has a right to know her mother but I am afraid if I find her she won't be Jewish or Catholic or whatever. What if she is this or that? I can't face that so..."* The number of excuses and explanations is infinite.

In order to get to know your child you must be prepared to

unconditionally love. I suppose if you are not ready to do that, there might be real wisdom in refusing to become involved.

Explaining these feelings to somebody who hasn't ever been through the adoption/reunion process seems impossible. On the other hand, we all go through some kind of loss in our lives because of death or rejection or something that has nothing to do with us. I've heard people talk about the loss of their home because of fire or a catastrophic financial reversal. That experience may be almost as painful as giving up a child. I don't know. I don't have anything to gauge that by because I gave up a child.

Depth of despair is only measurable by an individual person's response. Everyone handles things differently. There is really no right and wrong to feelings. The bottom line is that whatever happens, it is really is the way you deal with the circumstance rather than the circumstance itself that dictates the outcome.

The day that I decided to give Cat a chance for life in a whole family was the same day I found out for certain that I was pregnant. I recall it vividly. I did not begin to recover from that choice until the day that I actually saw her, and was able to put my arms around her. I never felt completely okay or completely whole until then. Only then did the cave in my heart start to fill in. I am not going to say it is the easiest thing in the world to repair. If you have ever knocked a scab off a wound, you may understand the feeling.

"Hey I am bleeding again." The wound has to be cleaned. Without attention any festering under the surface could cause gangrene to set in and kill you. It is a painful process. The deep sadness, chronic and deeper than depression, called grief, rose to the surface.

Cat was privileged to meet both of her birth parents. Her father and I went to see her one time together, to celebrate her birthday. From JH's point of view it was a precious gift. He wanted Cat to have the opportunity to see the two of us together. It was important to him that she knew we had meant a lot to each other. He was an adopted child who never met or even identified his father. JH has said many times how grateful he would be to look across the table one time at *"dear old dad."*

It turned out to be painful for Cat because JH really did not desire to have a day-to-day relationship with her. Even though she knows who he is and knows there are other siblings, she has not had any integration with that side of her heritage and it bothers her. I have talked to Cat many times about her feelings. I have tried to encourage her to recognize that what we get is a gift and to be thankful for what we have and not sorrowful for what we don't have. I have always felt it was up to JH to make his own choice. Like all of us, he will have to live with his decision. I deeply regret Cat's pain.

While everything between Cat and me is not perfect it mimics any other relationship between mother and child. People are people and no matter what, there is probably some place you have missed the mark as a parent. And as a child, there is probably is some area where you misunderstood your parent's intentions. Now that my children are all grown, I can look back and see that children and parents never have the same memories. I feel a responsibility to tell the people who are looking for their adopted children and/or birth parents that it can be a positive experience.

Foundational in the development of a relationship between two estranged relatives is the idea of familiarity. There is the thought that even though we don't know each other at all; we intrinsically know everything there is to know about the other one. At some psychological level we may be drawn to and repelled by each other at the same time. The deep connection at the spiritual or gut level resembles a magnetic field. There is polar attraction and yet if like poles become too close, they repel to a safe distance.

When Cat came back into my life, it was the greatest gift I

had ever gotten from God other than the gift of salvation and my other children. Her place in my heart doesn't take away one bit from the family that raised her.

Her adoptive parents are her *"MOM and DAD."* I call myself B-Ma. Sometimes I mean *Bonnie-Ma* and sometimes I mean *Birth-Ma.* Cat resembles me and our personalities are similar. We often see things the same way. An absolutely wonderful proof of the depths of the genetic pool, are some of our common characteristics.

We have come to realize that we love each other and are very important to one another. Our lives are richer for knowing each other. I love Cat. I love my granddaughter, Caity. I am very thankful and very proud that they are in my life. I foresee a lot of good times ahead and acceptance from each other in different ways. It is as complicated as our individual complex personalities.

My granddaughter has two grandmothers, like most kids, but it is unusual to have two grandmothers on your mother's side. Caity is eleven years old now and the day will come when she will start asking questions. One day she'll understand more fully what it means that her mommy was adopted. She'll realize what it means that her mother searched to find her birth mother. Caity is going to want to know, *"Hey, Grandma Bon-Bon why did you give away mommy?"* Maybe she will understand the answers to that tough question, if she can read this book. Hopefully, at least it will give us a place to start a meaningful dialog.

19

WESTWARD HO!

J ust before finishing this story I went to visit Cat and Caity in Colorado. Five years had passed since I last saw them. I had lost my job in the mental health field when the agency I worked for closed. I had started a new career as a freelance writer and had to put every bit of money and effort into that new endeavor. I couldn't wait to see them. This was my first trip to Denver and I was looking forward to seeing a little of Colorado as well.

Cat had been living in the Denver area a few years. She literally fled Pennsylvania to get away from Steve, her abusive ex-husband. After their divorce became final she moved to the United States Virgin Islands to make a new start for Caity and her. I never made it to visit them while they were in the Virgin Islands for a variety of reasons, so the last visit was before their move. They had stopped by in Melbourne to see Sara and me for a few days before they left.

I think they lived there approximately three years. Both Cat and Caity loved the beach and the warm island paradise. Cat earned a living using her talent for photography and has many beautiful pictures she brought back from there. Caity went to a

Montessori school where she had many enriching learning experiences, including learning to sail.

There was about a year when Cat and I had very little correspondence. Cat seldom answered my letters or phone calls. We have restored a dialog again, but not nearly as free flowing as it once had been. Cat told me that she had pulled back from all her family members in order to decide where the players fit. She also expressed anger with JH's lack of interest. I felt she was holding me partially responsible for his behavior and that was blocking our communication. I felt Cat was experiencing deep resentment.

The only way I know to solve a problem is to confront it, get it out into the open, define it and deal with it. So, I called up Cat and asked her if I could come out to Colorado to see her and Caity. I planned to stay with her because I thought it would give us a chance to talk things through and find the closeness we once had. I had talked it over with Sara and she agreed with me that the best way to find out what was going on was to see first hand.

Sara had gone to visit a few months before me and she really enjoyed herself. She wanted me to spend time with Caity and mend fences with Cat. It's not that we were not talking at all; it was just that we seemed to be at an invisible impasse.

I had mixed feelings as I went. Sometimes even the best relationship is very hard. Communication can go awry with little effort. Family is so important. Like Cat had explained about trying to fit all the players into their proper places in her life, I also felt like my entire entourage had been put into a blender. I feel betrayed and disappointed by events that had nothing to do with Cat. I was angry and sad with other family members. I realized it may not be the best timing for me emotionally. I was at a low point. But, it was done. The reservations were made and I was packed.

I know it is superficial of me but I wanted to look my best

and I have put on so much weight it is hard for me to see her. But, I am going. I had to swallow a lot of my feelings to go and face the music. I knew Cat and I needed to talk through a few things. I was uncertain of the root of the problem but I had been a co[...] the signs of a person with a gru[...]

[...] called just bef[...] t was still a goo[...] not great at wo[...] to postpone my[...] n each other fo[...]

[...] me up as she ha[...] le in to Long-m[...] point in front o[...] her house and v[...] e, I knew I was i[...] of her family members, two p[...] ven an iguana. I looked all over the house. There was not one picture of me to be seen anywhere, not even in my granddaughter's bedroom. I was the invisible grand-ma, I guess. That tugged at my heart and hurt me so much I was never able to even bring it up, which is unusual for me.

The two-week visit was difficult for all of us. I kept trying to reach out to Cat but no matter what I said, I felt like I was hitting a brick wall. I can't speak for Cat so I don't know if she felt the same. Cat was under a great deal of tension due to work problems and I am sure that was part of it. We hadn't seen each other for a long time and were struggling to communicate on the same wave length. I was tired and suffered from a bit of altitude sickness that left me feeling shaky and weak.

There was a definite difference in this visit from any other I had ever had with her. The tension was great. Cat had to work and was having trouble getting time off. I felt there were many things left unsaid that would have been best brought into the open, but the timing was wrong. Several unexpected events had increased Cat's stress level and she was not able to talk to me about anything I considered important. We needed to get to know each other again. Cat told me a little of what was bothering her and apologized. I also apologized for my part in the misunderstanding.

My last full day in Colorado Cat, Caity and I spent a wonderful day in Estes Park, a resort town in high in the Rockies, about forty minutes from Cat's home. We had been there twice before during the two weeks and I really enjoyed the drive through the mountains and was eager to see it again. The town is filled with wildlife in the spring. Elk and mule deer come down from higher elevations to feed on the new vegetation. We sat outside Starbuck's and drank a cup of coffee while watching the elk munch on the grass. Caity decided she wanted to try the climbing wall at a local mountain gear outlet. I took pictures of her about 25 feet in the air supported only by small hand and footholds. She is a natural athlete and very agile.

The *Ducky Derby*, an annual fund raising event done by the local service and non-profit agencies, was in full force when we arrived. Several thousand yellow plastic ducks were released into the river and *raced* for prizes. Each duck cost twenty dollars and the proceeds went to charity. It provided a wonderful excuse for locals and visitors alike to gather for dancing, drinking and good old-fashioned fun. We got a good laugh, had some food and drove back home.

One evening we went to a dog show at the Hotel Stanley in Estes. This famous hotel was the perfect setting to show the Great Pyrenees breed, a beautiful large canine related to the St. Bernard. I had never been to a dog show and was unfamiliar with the Great Pyrenees before I met the one Cat and Caity were *doggie sitting* with. I fell in love with these huge but gentle creatures. Another day Cat and I came back and walked through the museum at *The Stanley* where the mini-series of Stephen King's *The Shining* was filmed.

Building memories takes time and patience. Like other mothers and daughters, Cat and I share many traits. Some are good, some bad. I still believe it is a miracle that we were reunited. It is my desire to be in both Cat and Caity's lives until the day I die. I hope Cat finds lasting happiness and I will do what I can to help her, even leaving her alone if she wishes.

Cat and I also have many differences that may not ever be resolved. Her environment shaped her as mine had shaped me. Both heredity and environment play strong roles in personality development. Cat and I come from a different place. We have few shared experiences. Somehow that is not as important to me as being in her life and being able to share in my granddaughter's formative years. You cannot completely recapture the past. It is not even desirable to try. The best you can hope for is to be able to look to the future with hopeful anticipation.

The time came for me to leave. They drove me into Denver so I could stay overnight at a motel close to the airport. Saying goodbye was hard because I wasn't sure when we would see each other again. I felt we hadn't really made the connection I was hoping for. As I was hugging her, I was aware of her tension and didn't know how to make it better.

I looked into the face of the little girl I had never known.

"I love you", I said

"I love you too," said Cat, "I hope you know that."

COMING:

THE CIRCLE IS COMPLETE
VOLUME TWO IS COMING SOON

If you enjoyed reading about Cat and Bonnie's reunion and subsequent relationships with the entire family, we invite you to continue reading about a further chapter in our lives.

VOLUME TWO--JOHN

Although John F. (my son's name) is chronologically older than Cat by three years he did not search for me until about 12 years later than she did.

Cat had found me in 1991 and John first came into the family in 2003.

Volume One ends when Caity is 11 years old in 2002.

One evening in 2003 a woman's voice on the phone asked me if I knew (me,) Bonnie. She said she was from Penn State.

"I don't know where to begin," she said. "But I got this strange inquiry from a young man who thinks you might be his birth mother.

"Oh," I said, "Don't be distressed. It probably is my long lost son who I gave up for adoption back in the 60s. This is a wonderful surprise."

With that she relaxed and told me a little about what they had received. I asked her to mail me the material and told her she could pass on my phone number and address if he called back.

Cat had been 24 years old when she found me and I was 46. By the time John F. came into the picture I was 58 and he was age 40. I recall the first time we spoke he said, "Don't worry we will have the second forty years to get to know each other."

The first time I met him, John F came to Tennessee and spent time with me at my son and daughter-in-law's home outside of Nashville. As of today it is 16 years into the relationship. John F. has met most all the other players in the family.

When John F. was born I was 18 years old, and alone I went into labor and it was a time when the unwed pregnant woman was a real pariah. The attending nurses did everything to make sure I would remember my "sin."

It was by the grace of God that he found his siblings and me.

I hope you will read the continuation of our saga. It will explain a lot of the gaps and hopefully make the story more understandable.

John F. looks like my father.

ACKNOWLEDGMENTS

NOTE FROM THE AUTHOR

This is, after all, my story, full of my feelings and in the context
of the early 1960s and the 50s in which I was raised. I was 18 in
1962. I came from a time before women's liberation, when
sexual expression was limited to wondering what *it* was like and
talking to girlfriends about petting.

I cannot speak for any other birth mother or pretend to
know their feelings. However, I have spoken to many women in
the course of my preparation to write this book, during counseling sessions as a mental health professional, and to friends
who confessed their *"secret"* over the years. Many become
tearful and still bear enormous pain. To give birth, in the 50s,
60s and early 70s as single woman, to an illegitimate child, was
a serious breach of acceptable behavior and the subject of many
a gossip session. There were *homes* where girls were sent to hide
the *family's shame.*

Young women would return back to *normal* after a
prolonged *visit* with some distant relative. The information was
not even shared with close friends or relatives. It was a dark

secret. The pretense was so great that virginity was faked on *"The Wedding Night."*

I have listened to women who were so fearful of rejection, they dared not even tell their husband or their other children. Women, who continue to suffer in silence, never know the fate of their child and expect nothing.

I have also *been there* for a friend's daughter in the 1990's who became pregnant and found out *too late* for an abortion. This teenager named the baby after me and was able to choose the mother (a single parent) that she desired to raise her child. It was all in the open and a much healthier way to approach life.

I know the adoption climate is different now.

Recently a young girl testified in my Church about her pregnancy and decision to give up her child for adoption to a loving couple and she was applauded for her courage. Today, the birth mother is seen as a heroine who, by giving someone a child instead of having an abortion, is rewarded as a doing the *right* thing.

The condemnation for the out-of-marriage sexual involvement is not even part of the equation today as it once was. I am glad for this trend in one way. It is hard enough to surrender your own flesh, without enduring the societal stigma that was part of the experience for a birth mother in my era.

ADDENDUM

The Face of Adoption Today

Shortly after Cat came to visit in Florida the first time, a young woman who was about the same age as my son and daughter-in-law, told me that she had given up a baby a few years earlier. She said it encouraged her to see Cat and me together. This young woman had not been reunited with her child, because he was still only about five years old. The experience had been very traumatic for her, even though she had done an *open adoption*. She did have expectations that she will meet her child eventually. She was still thankful to have someone to talk to about the adoption and her sense of loss. Although she felt hopeful that she and her child would have a chance to get to know each other, she still felt the pain and grief of the separation.

After meeting Cat, one of my closest friends disclosed that she had also given up a daughter for adoption. Like me, she had not shared the story before. They had never been reunited. Several other women close to my age came forward to talk with me. Even though each circumstance differed, these strangers all told similar stories that contained number of mon threads. None of the women felt like they had the right or the courage to find their children, and they had not been found. In each face I saw profound sadness. I felt the unresolved grief.

One mother and son, Charlotte and Jeff, who had just been re-united, began coming to our church. They closely resembled each other, like Cat and me. It was fun to watch them together, as both were very happy to have each other. They were excited for Cat and me. Unfortunately, due to the distance, Cat never met them, but I spent time with Charlotte and Jeff and the whole birth/adoptive family mix. They were really the only people I knew who were dealing with all the different emotions.

Our lives and our stories differed a great deal. Charlotte had left her family to move within a few miles of Jeff and stayed about two years until she felt her family was sufficiently integrated. After that she was ready to have a more normal relationship. Her husband and children came to visit and supported her as she worked through all the issues. It was an exceptional case.

I did not know how to behave or decipher my feelings. There was nowhere to go nor was there anything to read that talked much beyond the *re-union experience*. There wasn't any adoption group in my area that dealt with birth parents being re-united, and what happens next. Even my well-meaning friends, unless they had experienced the same thing, could not seem to grasp the enormity of having a new adult child join the family. I had *come out of the closet* and despite all the support groups for most every other situation, there was nothing available to help frame a modus operandi.

I sought help at one of the local adoption agencies. Even framing the question proved difficult. When I asked for help for a birth mother I was told there was counseling available for the currently pregnant. Help was offered to birth mothers and fathers making the decision and logistics to give up a child for adoption. There was no support group for birth parents trying to cope with being found or finding their children and the aftermath of such a traumatic event.

It was good for me to talk to birth mothers even if they had not been reunited with their children because it helped me to realize that *"Hey, there are a lot of us out here"*, especially that gave up children for adoption in the sixties or before. There was no discussion of choice; you gave up your baby, period. Then you walked away and *forgot it*. Charlotte described having her son literally ripped out of her arms because at age fifteen she had no say in the decision. Her parents made the choice.

There were homes that specialized in hiding unwed mothers and, no question, it was a "family secret." You went away, at your parent's insistence, had your baby, and went on with your life. It seems incredibly barbaric now, but when I was that age and pregnant the two alternatives were marriage or adoption. Of course there was no abortion, and very few actually kept their children, that was just not done. If you kept you child you risked the word *'bastard'* applied to your child quite freely. Actually those of us with middle class upbringing were really geared to give the baby up for adoption in order that the baby would have an opportunity to grow up in a home with two parents. Let's face it, an unmarried mother never joined the cast of *"Leave it to Beaver."* One cannot picture Ward Cleaver dealing with that, no matter what a great dad he was.

Back in the fifties and early sixties the idea was that if you had a baby you wouldn't be able to get a man. You wouldn't be able to have a family, and you would be all alone for the rest of your life. There was sometimes a stigma attached to the adopted child as there was one attached to a child who was illegitimate. Some children were never told they were adopted until they were grown up. A few only found out after the death of their parents.

Additionally, it was thought that the baby would be cheated out of a decent up bringing. Research from that era stressed the *consequences* of single parent families. Statistics from sociological studies *proved* that *juvenile delinquents* were more prevalent in single parent homes. Children raised in a one-parent environment were headed to jail, drugs and whatever other *bad* end you could imagine.

Being a single parent continued to be a major source of guilt for me even while I raised my other children in the seventies and eighties despite the changing social mores. It was especially embarrassing for me to tell Cat I had been divorced three times. In the twenty-first century this seems like an archaic idea, but before the sexual revolution, women's lib and an almost sixty percent divorce rate, single parenting was not accepted as an alternative family. In retrospect, I would never have given up Cat.

I did talk to a few adoptees that had also stepped forward once they knew I was a birth mom. Their experience gave me some insight into what it was like to be an adopted child. Although every family is unique there are common issues that helped to better understand what I was dealing with.

Most of my research is experiential, based on the number of individuals I have met that are adopted or have given up children for adoption. Some have reunited with their children, others will or won't based on whatever reason they find. Some birth parents have met their children but don't desire to have a relationship. Adoptees may only want to know whom they look like or get a medical history. The range of curiosity varies from those who are not terribly interested to those whose lives seem empty without knowing their roots. Both birth parents and adoptees may feel angry or disappointed whether they meet each other or not.

I felt my situation was somewhat unique. Not too many people stay in more than superficial contact. But, as far as I know, there are no statistics on how many birth parents and children reunite. How would you measure the *success rate*? Is there a correlation between reunion and length of acquaintance? I know of many occasions where birth mother met with child one time. Both sides received closure, and were satisfied. On other occasions, the child and birth parent may have met once or twice and a desire to continue in the relationship was not agreeable to both sides. That hurtful scenario appears to be the norm rather than the unusual. But, we do not have any statistics to support that kind of theory about adoption reunions.

I am speaking about the adoption of children who are thirty to fifty years old now. They are the children born in the fifties and sixties. Laws have changed to allow many kinds of adoption not in existence prior to the eighties, at least not in the formalized sense. Single parent adoption was unheard of, couples over forty were told they were *too old*, interracial adoption was almost non-existent, and homosexual placement was not even considered. Special needs children generally remained in institutional settings.

Adoption is not about abandonment. The process of adoption in the twenty-first century barely resembles what I experienced in the nineteen sixties. Jo Ann Welch, a Licensed Clinical Social Worker (LCSW) is an adoption professional for Gift of Life, Inc., a private agency in Florida. Welch has thirty years of experience in the field.

"What was missing in the sixties was the ability to understand and help the birth mother work through the grief process," said Welch. *"We thought it was the kindest thing to get the mother through the birth, tell her to forget it, and go on with her life The birth mom was not given a choice, merely guided through what was already decided for her. In 1968 and before, there were no adoption plans."*

Today's adoption professionals need to do two things with our birth parents and adoptive families. First, we have an obligation to our birth moms to help them develop and understand the choice and plan. We need to educate about grief, which is a normal part of loss. We must also help our birth parents understand that recognizing the grief process in no way takes away the pain, but it does allow for healing. The second part of our responsibility is the help adoptive parents change their language so they can present the adoption experience in a more positive way. There must be an adoption story that explains that the birth mother loved her child enough to make a plan in the child's best interest. Telling an adoptive child that they were 'given away' somehow implies they were less than perfect."

Today a birth mother is encouraged to choose the adoptive family she wants for her child. The birth mother and adoptive family meet and discuss the degree of openness they desire. Choices for adoption run from the totally closed to the totally open. The degrees of closed or openness range from no contact to day-to-day contact between the adoptive family and the birth mother, with her as part of the family unit. The birth mother and the adoptive mother may even be in the delivery room together for a shared birth experience that may be passed along to the child.

Openness is on a continuum. Most birthparent /adoptive family relationships fall somewhere in the center. According to Welch an adoptive family who wants to work with *Gift of Life, Inc.* for adoption within the United States must be willing to send pictures to the birth mom four times the first year and once a year after that until the child is age twelve. But, there is also a clear understanding on both sides that the adoptive parents' role will never be usurped. If a couple desires a totally closed adoption, there are often opportunities for them to adopt foreign children.

Today's climate is certainly a *"kinder, gentler"* approach for both birth parent and child. In Florida there is an Adoption Registry that will allow adoptive children who have reached age eighteen easy access to their birth records.

ABOUT THE AUTHOR

BONNIE L. QUICK, BSW, MPA

After the birth of Cat, Bonnie Quick went on with her life. Quick spent over twenty years in the mental health field. After she earned her Bachelor of Arts in Social Welfare from the Pennsylvania State University, she worked in a clinic setting as a counselor. She earned her Master's from Troy State University while a single mother. Her thesis, *Middle Class Indigence,* examines the plight of the suddenly single person whose income is affected by divorce or death of significant other.

Quick served as Program Director of *The Displaced Homemakers*, Director of *Focus on Women*, an addiction and recovery program, and Facilitator of *The Domestic Violence Intervention Program*, an education program for offenders. She testified before the *Governor's Gender Bias Committee* in Pensacola, which resulted in changes in the Florida judicial system.

Quick raised two children, a boy and a girl. She is the proud grandmother of four granddaughters. She lives in Florida with her faithful companion, Mr. Kitty.

Quick is now pursuing her childhood dream to write and she freelances for a variety of publications while working on other books and projects. She hopes to facilitate a support group for birthmothers one day.

If a birthmother, adoptee or someone else touched by this issue would like to contact Quick, she would welcome an email: blqwriter@gmail.com

Quick is also available to speak to your organization or group.

f

ARTICLES

It was after I had written this article that I began to work on the book.

I have since written a few more and have spoken at three conferences on behalf of the birth mother experience.

ADOPTION-
A Birth Mother's Point of View

There is possibly nothing quite as empty as a mother who has just given birth to a baby she knows she cannot take home. There is no amount of comfort or consolation anyone or anything can offer that acts to prevent the feelings of intense grief and sense of loss. There are not enough tears to soothe the eyes or hugs to dull the longing.

The fact that a conscious choice was made to give up the child to a "whole" family does not alter the consequence of separation. I recall looking at a vase, filled only with its cloudy water, empty of the flowers that had recently occupied that space and totally identifying with it. I was an empty vessel without my precious baby. Postpartum depression was large and real.

How can I tell you what it felt like to me to hold my tummy as I walked, caressing the contents from the outside, wishing the time would never come? I would talk to her--somehow I was always sure it was a girl--and tell her I loved her.

She was born on All Saints Day, which for me, was as ironic a birth date as possible. I felt I had been plunged into the depths of hell. I wept and went on.

The resulting ambivalence that set in, allowed life to go on. There was my intellect telling me that I *did the right thing.* It was a perfectly good lie and worked well most of the time. But then there were those damnable birthdays, holidays, and special occasions like subsequent pregnancies to jerk the bottle of pain off the shelf. Somehow the stopper came out, and the empty ache filled me like the Genie from Aladdin filled the room. However, this time there was no choice of wishes. Only one thing emerged. Exquisite agony! Acute enough to bring me to my knees. I felt rage amidst the anguish.

Then, the day came I dared not expect even though for years I had prayed *"If I am looked for, Lord, let me be found."* A letter arrived. It was from *HER.* It started out *"This is the most important letter I have ever had to write."* Before I could even walk the half-acre back into the house, I read through to the end of the text to where the telephone number and address were. Next thing I knew I was dialing. It was busy for the first many tries. The wait seemed interminable. Finally, SHE answers.

"Hello, YOU have found me." I say.

She says to her husband who is in the background *"IT'S HER."*

It is funny that no further explanation of identity beyond *"SHE or HER"* was necessary as voices that talked back and forth to one another were similar enough to be familiar. One phone conversation followed another.

Arrangements were made for me to board a plane and fly into ABE. My daughter was waiting and the video camera recorded the event. We hugged and she handed me white roses.

Mother and child are re-united. Eyes looked into eyes that are so similar it is like looking in a mirror. Both said, *"You are so beautiful."* and really meant it. Joy unspeakable and full of glory!

The first few days of our first visit were a supermarket of information exchange. It took weeks to process all of it. We stared at each other and compared hands and feet. We devoured family albums as I answered questions about her two siblings. She had a few photos that I could not put down. We smiled a lot and each made a pact not to waste a minute of our precious time together by crying. That came later as we both wept for days after we said good-bye. But, now the tears brought with them happiness and healing.

It was amazing to find out our similarities in attitudes, personality traits and even tastes in furniture and other items. Both of us are eclectic in our likes and dislikes and strong-willed. We discovered a common characteristic of seldom completing a sentence. Maybe because people tend to interrupt so much, who knows? Several times we finished each other's sentences or said the same word.

I felt whole for the first time in my adult life. She said "The circle is complete." when she called me about the birth of my granddaughter. As I held the baby and looked into my adult child's face, it was like being in a time machine capable of allowing existence in two time zones at once. I held my baby granddaughter and it was her mother also.

In the past eight years we have maintained a close relationship. We are mother and daughter. I did not replace, but rather augment, the mother who raised her. We have cried with each other, hugged, yelled at each other, made up and shared great times with each other. We have become friends who have enriched each other's lives. No matter what happens in the future we will be there for one another.

We love each other. We are family. No greater gift has ever been given.

(This was originally published by The Morning Call, Allentown, PA. Lehigh Valley Woman Magazine, winter 1999)

Made in the USA
Lexington, KY
28 October 2019